THE *Love*, *Heartache*, AND
Devotion OF A MOM AND GRANDMA
♥ ♥ ♥

The *Love*, *Heartache*, and *Devotion* of a Mom and Grandma

♥♥♥

STORY OF A VERY STRONG FAITH AND HOPE!

DARCIE JOY MILLER

XULON PRESS

Xulon Press
2301 Lucien Way #415
Maitland, FL 32751
407.339.4217
www.xulonpress.com

Printed in the United States of America.

Paperback ISBN-13: 978-1-6322-1139-2
Hard Cover ISBN-13: 978-1-6322-1140-8
eBook ISBN-13: 978-1-6322-1141-5

Dedication

I dedicate this book to my children and all my grand-children! You have witnessed my frustration and my passion firsthand, and many times my mind and energy might have been involved in what was happening at the time. Always know I loved each and every one of you and tried very hard to do my best to be there for all of you. Also to all the children that are out there, suffering in abusive and neglectful situations with parents who are also suffering in their own pain from sexual abuse, mental illness, and addictions, I pray that we can do a better job to address issues sooner—instead of later for everyone. I also would like to dedicate this book to all grandparents and family out there who are trying to be a voice, advocating to help their children and grandchildren. Never fail to stand up for the little children and grandchildren you love, as they often cannot speak for themselves. You will never be sorry that you helped these children to have a better life, even if it creates uncomfortable situations with your own child—their parent. Enabling your adult child by not seeing the truth and calling out serious concerns only continues to create more problems and continues the dysfunctional behaviors into the next generation.

I have shared more in my book than I had originally planned. I hope in doing so, I have given a *voice* to both my daughter and my grandson who have passed away and also to my other three grandchildren who have lived through this nightmare. They were too young to really speak for themselves or if they did, no one listened. I also want to give a voice for grandparents, especially grandmas, who often have to witness all of these things while loving both their adult child—the parent—and loving and trying to protect your precious grandchildren! I truly understand and feel your heartache.

Praises For "The Love, Heartache, and Devotion of a Mom and Grandma!"

- Throughout the book, the author effectively maintains an uplifting voice of encouragement and positivity without shying away from the reality of the author's past experiences, choosing to share the author's ability to overcome challenges and embrace the blessings of the present. The author's voice and tone of the book inspire the reader, through both a spirit of positivity and the realism and vulnerability within the text. —**Xulon Editor**
- Within the writing, the author provides a strong balance of sharing real-life experiences with practical and spiritual teaching so that the reader can benefit from both the author's experiences and teaching that they can apply to their own life. The author's teaching is relatable, realistic, and applicable, helping the reader overcome similar situations in their personal journey. —**Xulon Editor**
- The author beautifully ties up the end of the book, with a solid conclusion in which the reader gains access into the author's present-day life as well as the author's heart of compassion, love, and grace. This conclusion reiterates to the reader the importance of God's presence in one's spiritual journey through life. —**Xulon Editor**

Table of Contents

Chapter 1

Growing Up as a Child

I was born in a small rural town in the Midwest back in 1948, the oldest of three children. My dad, Meryl, and my mom, Fran, were both very loving parents to all of us kids. My mom was especially loving, and I was secure in the love expressed through many hugs and kisses through both sides of our families. My dad was not overly involved, but that was very common back in those days, as it was more the duty of the mother to raise the children and the father to go to work. My mom did a good job, as a full-time mom, and my father always held a job. We always felt loved and safe and were well taken care of. We did not have a lot of money, as my mom was a stay-at-home mom for most of my young life. We had many extended family involved in our lives, who loved us. I feel I had a very good childhood, despite not having a father who was involved much in my life.

Before my parents were married, my dad had served in World War II—right out of high school at the age of seventeen. I'm sure my dad had seen many horrible things as a very young man, which affected him over his life, and later I realized that this part of his young life could have led him to deal with these issues by turning to alcohol. After his return from the war, my parents were married, and they started their family. A couple years after I was born, my sister, Sandy, was born, and five years later, my baby brother, Mark, was born.

My parents were a very nice-looking couple and well liked in our small town—and we kids were well liked. My dad was a hard worker and a good dad—when he was around, anyway. My dad would show us love and affection, and he also made us respect and listen to our mom when he was and wasn't at home. My dad was an over-the-road truck driver, and he had two very serious addictions—alcohol and women.

Throughout our early lives, my siblings and I witnessed much emotional hurt he caused our mom, as she had to endure many embarrassing, hurtful times my dad displayed in this small town. Our dad was very seldom available to us, as he often chose his free time to be spent in taverns with his friends and with women, some being my mom's friends. Unfortunately, my dad found this more important than being involved with his wife and children. One of our most hurtful times would always fall on Christmas Eve when my mom would go to great lengths, preparing food and presents to enjoy with my dad's family— only to have my dad show up very late, having been drinking. I remember the many disappointments we all felt as very young children—and the deep hurt that was caused to our mom.

Future Christmas celebrations with my dad, with my own children, would oftentimes end in the same disappointments and hurt for me and my children. My dad would come late and drunk, or get drunk and leave our home—reminding me of my younger years. Eventually I would not allow it anymore, which would lead to my dad getting very upset with me.

There was one Christmastime in particular that I remember; my dad had left our house with my stepmom, and I almost called the police on him. I feared that he would get in an accident because he was so drunk, as he would be traveling on the highway for about an hour to get home. I was concerned that he could possibly hurt or kill someone. You see as old as he was, he had not learned to not drink when he was driving. You would have thought that a past serious accident years ago that almost killed him and three other people would have taught him that lesson, but it hadn't.

Back in those days, these kinds of issues were not dealt with seriously, and oftentimes the police and sheriff's department, especially in a small town in the county, would let people off because they had a family, so my dad never had to face any consequences for his serious drinking problem. I am very thankful that today we have laws and are addressing these issues much sooner and with consequences, hoping to improve situations for families.

I am also very thankful there was not domestic violence when my dad was drinking—as my dad was a happy, more sickening drunk. Only once did I hear a fight. Of course, my mom usually never confronted him, but there was this one time that she did. There was much emotional abuse, though, and it was very much damaging to my mom—as my dad openly womanized out in public in front of my mom and us kids. Instead of my mom getting mad at my dad, my mom oftentimes would let it pass just so she could be with my dad—and then look at what she wasn't doing right, blaming herself.

I loved my dad, but I never respected him, and I oftentimes did not realize why my mom did not hold him more accountable and confront him. My mom would internalize the hurt she was going through and then become depressed as time went on, which affected her more in her later years as she looked back on her life.

At the very early age of ten years old I seemed to understand more than I should have—figuring things out way beyond my years as to what was going on. One time, my dad had the guts to take us three kids on a family outing with our mom to a bar/restaurant out of town to eat, where his current girlfriend was working. Nice family outing, don't you think? For some reason, at the young age of ten, I suspected this lady was way too nice to my dad and us kids, and I later found out the reason why. That was when she showed up to visit our dad in the hospital after his terrible car accident the following winter!

Sometimes my dad would call me, when my children were younger, and ask for money, and if I told him, "No, I won't give you money, but I will buy you a meal or put gas in your car," he would get so upset. He would say, "You and your sister, Sandy, living in your nice houses up on the hill. He was accusing us of having a nice place to live when he didn't, trying to make us feel guilty.

I had learned my lesson of not enabling my dad. One time I had given him twenty-five dollars because he called so desperate to have money to get something to eat and gas for his car. A few days later, after talking with my sister and my aunt Becky, Dad's sister, to find out they had also given my dad money after hearing the same story. So in that one day, my dad had manipulated us into giving him quite a bit of money to spend, probably most of it on alcohol. It was then that I vowed to always love my dad but never enable him again. As time went on, we kids tried to do a couple interventions for my dad to get him the help he needed, but nothing ever seemed to work as there was always another woman or person to give him money or a place to live with no responsibility or consequences.

Like I said, my dad could be very loving and caring—a special memory of us together was he would occasionally take me with him when he drove the big gas truck and let me go up on top and check to see when it was empty. My dad sometimes would drive this gas truck when he was drinking. Thank God, he was never in an accident. My dad had his own band along with my grandpa, and my dad's dream was for me to play the accordion in his band someday, but it wasn't something I really wanted to do. I did have an accordion and did take lessons and I learned to play it, but I never played in his band, so my dad's dream of this never did happen.

I have very many special memories of my mom. She always made our Christmas' very special, as well as our birthdays. Even though money was not plentiful, we always had the necessities and were always well taken care of and dressed well—and loved! My aunt Loretta, Mom's sister, helped my mom a lot with clothes for us kids and the extras that sometimes were needed. My mom's older sister had lost her husband very early in her life, and she never remarried or had any children of her own, so we became almost like her children. Although she lived a couple hours away, she was a very important part of our lives. I'm sure my mom went without things for herself often because my dad would rather use his paychecks for entertainment for himself and his friends, buying a round of drinks at the local tavern for everyone on payday. We had another two sets of aunts and uncles who lived an hour away and also had no children— sisters of my mom—that also were often there for my mom to help financially.

Being raised in a small town, there wasn't much in the town to do or places to go, except of course to taverns, better known as bars today. Often on Friday and Saturday nights, it was commonplace for our family and many families to hang out at one of the two taverns in our town. The parents were in the bars socializing and dancing, and the town kids were outside playing kick the can or hide and seek on the main street in our town. My sister and I were sometimes made to dance with older men in bars as young children, and we hated it. My dad thought it was cool as he bragged about "his girls" and how proud he was of us. We were very thankful nothing ever happened to us as these men were drunk. Everyone knew everybody and of course also knew everyone's business. People could also be very cruel in a small town and very judgmental, as I will share with you later an experience I had.

I had been baptized as an infant in a small church in this town, and I attended Sunday school, as a young child—so I was a Christian early on in my life—although we rarely attended church together as a family. I would be so embarrassed on some Sunday mornings as a child, coming home from Sunday school or church to have my dad and his friends sitting out-side drinking at a couple different houses where we lived. These houses were close by one of our churches where many people from our small town would drive by. Living in a small town, everyone knew who lived there and what was going on—and of course would share with others.

As kids, we walked to school from across town, about a mile, and my sister, Sandy, and I had paper routes. We went to a small school where we had many friends, but our parents weren't much involved with school or outside things with us kids. Again, I think that was pretty common back in that time. Every other weekend or at least once a month, on Sunday, my mom would take us kids over to see her parents—our grandparents—and oftentimes our aunts, uncles, and cousins were there. Our grandparents lived in another small town a few miles away. We kids would love sitting out on our grandparent's big front porch on their porch swing with our cousins and playing in their big side yard. My grandparents on my dad's side lived in our same town close by us. Our families all were very close, and we enjoyed being together and had fun doing very simple things!

I'm so thankful that I had very caring, loving grandparents. I have special memories of my maternal grandparents who were older, as my mom was the baby of the family. I really enjoyed going there. I would take the Greyhound bus on my own at age ten to stay overnight with them. I would sit with my grandma, Frieda, at the sewing machine, handing her material pieces for making a quilt. My grandfather, Fred, was a night watchman for this small town, and he worked during the night. I remember going out to his workshop and would watch him make things, like our doll furniture. Once in a while, we would get him to give us a ride in his Model T car, and we would ride in the rumble seat down the alley. As little kids we thought that was such a big deal—and so much fun!

They also had an outhouse, and we had to use a cold bedpan at night when we stayed in their cold upstairs. At their home they had to pump and heat water. They also had a very large garden. My grandparents were hard workers and did not spend much time entertaining themselves or others. I remember my grandma would fix a big meal for the whole family with two different shifts to eat at least once or twice a month when we would all come.

With my paternal grandparents living in our same small town, we saw them often. I would mow their large lawn, and I remember my grandpa, Hank, was always helping to move the large rocks along the border of their yard on this main highway through our town. I remember my sister, Sandy, and I would stay overnight and help to pop popcorn on the stove. We would also play the piano in their basement with our grandma, Evelyn, often saying to us, "Don't play the piano so loud."

As a young child, I do recall seeing alcohol as a big part of every get-together with both sides of my family. The first thing after you arrived at any family member's home, you were greeted and hugged—you were always hugged and kissed when you came and when you left someone's house—then the adults were asked what they wanted to drink. There was some social time before you would have a meal, and everyone seemed to have an alcoholic drink before we would sit down to eat. It was their social, relaxing time.

When I was eleven, my dad was in a serious automobile accident, involving alcohol, where he was the driver. Two vehicles were involved with two people in each car, and they were all in critical condition and almost died. This is when my mother found out about another woman in my dad's life. As my mom walked into the hospital room one day, she found her there. This was the final straw for my mom! She stayed with my dad until he was able to leave the hospital after several weeks, and could get back on his feet. Then she carried through with her plans to divorce him and move away from this town.

During this time, I also overheard a so-called friend of our family in this small town say about me, "She will never amount to anything coming from divorced parents." I thought to myself, *How dare she think that she can foretell my future at eleven years old.* She herself wasn't a real good example of responsible behavior, as she ran around on her husband/husbands and was the mother of five children. So she thought she could predict how I would turn out? What she didn't know was that what she had said about me had a very big impact on my life. What she had said did hurt me at the time, but that hurt would only help me over time to want to be more determined to make something of my life! I would prove her—and that small, gossiping town—wrong!

Also, during this time my girlfriend, Mary, and I would take turns staying at each other's houses on the weekend. One weekend, I was to stay at her house. As I look back, I believe God spoke to me and kept me from staying at my friend's house that night because her house was destroyed in a fire, and she and her parents narrowly escaped. For some reason I didn't want to stay that night—very unusual for me. What if I would have stayed that night at her farmhouse? Would we have stayed up later and been sleeping too soundly? Would my friend, Mary, have been awakened and been able to get her older parents up to have them all jump out an upstairs window to safety?

The end of that summer my mom moved us to a larger town, about an hour away, and divorced our dad. My mom was so very brave to take three young children, ages four, nine, and eleven, move from a small town out on her own to a larger city, get a full time job, and buy a house on her own. My mom knew no one in this town and had never worked a full-time job before! That was a giant step, especially back in those days when divorce was not common. It took becoming an adult to see and appreciate her bravery and strength. God must have given her amazing strength and courage through this very frightening time! She had a lot on her plate of full-time responsibility of three little children and a lot of financial demands with little to no monetary support from my dad. Back in those days, no automatic child support was given—and no government help. My dad always seemed to have better things to do with his money than to support his children. Occasionally if he would have money left over, he would send some to my mom, and occasionally if he had nothing better to do, he would come and visit us!

As a child, moving into junior high (what we call today's middle school), I was not very happy to have moved to this bigger town, changing schools and leaving all my friends in our small town. Even though there were more opportunities and things to do for us kids, we didn't like it at first. I gave my mom a hard time the first year or so, and looking back, I regret that I couldn't have been more understanding and willingly helpful. My mom was working a full-time job after having been able to stay home with us and working only part time. I was given a lot of responsibility to watch my sister, Sandy, and brother, Mark. I had to start a lot of the meals at eleven years old, and I kind of resented it. Even though I was very upset with my dad, I had a deep yearning for my parents to get back together. As I mentioned, back in those days, divorce was not common, and my mom was not treated too well—especially in the church— which was very sad.

During the days growing up as children, we lived pretty simply, as my dad did not add much income to our household. My mom often lived payday to payday, and there were no services out there to help single moms. My mom would not go to court to force my dad to pay. It seemed to me that we were not too important to him. My sister and I have often shared that we very easily could have looked for love in all the wrong places, as we really didn't ever have a dad who spent any time with us or showed us much attention and fatherly love, especially in our teen years.

Later, as I had my own children, my anger toward my dad grew because of his lack of involvement in our lives as children and then the continued lack of interest with my own children— his grandchildren—I wasn't sure how I would feel if he would ever get sick and need me. God was able to work in me and soften my heart when the time came, though.

One night, I was called and informed they had to perform an emergency tracheotomy on my dad. They found he had throat cancer, and they were giving him two months to live. It was then that my dad started to become a caring dad, wanting to really get to know his family. Maybe God was working also in my dad. He finally wanted to spend some quality time with us and care about us and our children, his grandchildren, before he died. God blessed my dad, and he was given some extra time. He lived for another year and a half and didn't actually die of the cancer. Our time spent together during this year and a half was the best it had ever been.

As kids we never wanted to hurt our mom any more than she had already been hurt, so we tried to make good choices throughout our teen years—most of the time, anyway! My sister and I both stayed away from alcohol and drugs and tried very hard to be responsible throughout our lives. Occasionally, I will have a drink but have always been very careful, as I know the serious history of the alcohol addiction in especially my dad's side of the family. My mom later married my stepdad, Dan, and he was very good to her and to us kids. He had three boys that he had pretty much raised as a single dad. My stepdad also was a drinker but not an alcoholic. I didn't truly realize how much he cared about us kids until he was gone, as he died fairly young of heart-related problems.

My husband, Paul, and I met when I was not quite sixteen, and we were married right after I graduated from high school at age eighteen—two weeks after my mom married my step dad—and three weeks after I graduated from high school. That was a very busy, crazy time! My goal in life was always to grow up and get married and have a family, so I was very happy!

Chapter 2

My Marriage and Family

y husband Paul and I were married in the Catholic church he belonged to on a very hot summer day in June. For the very first time in our area, my Protestant minister could share a prayer during the service. I had dreams of having that perfect marriage and family. We had our first child, a beautiful daughter, Danielle, when I was nineteen years old—born to us after we had been married for a year and a half. When I first saw my beautiful little chubby-cheeked daughter, after twenty-three hours of labor, I could see my maternal grandmother in her. I was so very happy to be a new mom! She was such a sweet, content baby—(and we named her right), as she would wake up at the crack of dawn—but would not cry and just look around. She was such an adorable baby and a very well-behaved little girl and a delight throughout the years. Many people would comment how adorable she was!

She did give us a real scare at a year and a half, though, when she was very sick with the flu and ran a very high fever and stopped breathing. A neighbor lady had just taken child CPR and was there to help until the ambulance came, as I was a basket case. She had what was called a fever convulsion and was a very sick little girl for a few days. For several years we had to watch her closely, whenever she would run the slightest fever, as this could happen again. As you can guess, I didn't sleep much at night during those years.

Danielle was a delightful little girl who loved to play with her many friends. As we've realized by looking back at old home movies, she also was quite a little character. Many of her friends spent lots of time at our home. She was an excellent student in school and was involved in dance, girl scouts, softball, band, track, and other school activities, while also working a part-time job in high school. She graduated from high school and went on to graduate college with a business degree, got married, and has one son. She was and is so very sweet and kind to everyone.

Our son, Shannon, was born almost four years later. The first couple of months, he was a pretty content little baby, but then for the next seven months, he wasn't! He didn't sleep more than fifteen minutes during the day and an hour at night from two to nine months. That was a very challenging time for me as a mom! When I held him, he always stood up on his feet from two months on—unless he was eating. He was so very strong that we had him walking around, putting weight on his feet, at two months old. I'm not kidding you! We were told at the hospital when he was born to never leave him lying on a table or bed alone because he tried to turn over shortly after being born. He certainly was a strong little guy! I'm thinking he would be a very early walker, but he was about average age when he started. He also didn't like riding in a car for longer than about ten minutes or so. He wore me out!

Once he was about nine months old and started getting around on his own, he was much more content. He wanted his independence! Imagine that, at less than a year? From then on he was such a sweet little boy and enjoyed working outside and helping out. In our neighborhood, he was called the "neighborhood news boy," as he would check out what was going on in the neighborhood every morning and share with all the neighbors. Our son was such a cute little boy! He was also very fascinated by the garbage truck and would help to bring the garbage cans back up by our house. Actually, he wanted to be a garbage man when he was a little boy, that is, until he happened to help take the garbage out one time and something leaked on his leg. At that point he no longer wanted to be a garbage man. He also was his dad's little helper outside when he was little, helping him build a retaining wall in our yard.

My son had many friends who played at our house, and he was an excellent student in school, involved in baseball, boy scouts, football, wrestling, and other school activities—and he also liked to ski. He went on to graduate high school and went on to college and to a very good job. He also married but later divorced and has two sons.

Our youngest daughter, Heidi, was born another five years after our son, and so our family was complete. She was a sweet baby—a good little girl—our sweet little angel and Daddy's little ladybug! She loved to play with her baby dolls and her cat, Snowball. I enjoyed holding each one of my children while I would feed them their bottles and also loved rocking them, oftentimes to sleep.

Early on I realized that my youngest daughter was not engaging with me like my other two children did and that she wasn't picking up on things quite as fast. But then, my older two kids were advanced for their age. However, they would say my youngest was falling within the lower end of normal range. I would ask questions, but no one was too concerned. So I tried not to worry and compare too much, and encouraged her and let her develop in her own time and in her own way. One thing

I did see when she was very young that scared me was her lack of fear of people, especially of men, boundaries, and places. She seemed to go up to the edges of walls without any fear of falling and would also go to strange men without hesitation. This concerned me very much!

As my husband and I look back on our experience with our youngest daughter and with the public school at an early age, we went from being good young parents of our two older children to all of a sudden being not-so-good parents. We believe as we look back and all the testing that was done—and the questions asked—that they might have suspected child abuse and that we might be the cause of what was going on. One time, we had a room full of highly educated people, trying to tell us about our child of six years old in kindergarten and the fact that she might never read. They were being so very hurtful and negative about the situation.

As our older children, Danielle and Shannon grew, and did very well in school, our youngest daughter, Heidi, continued to struggle. We were told later on by her psychologist that because her kindergarten experience was not good, it could have affected her throughout her entire school life. We moved her mid-kindergarten year to a private Christian school, and she did so much better. We kept her there through second grade and then moved her back to public school because our oldest daughter was starting college, and we were not able to afford to continue our youngest in private school and also pay for college. We also felt there were some programs available for Heidi in the public schools that could benefit her. This is a very major regret I have! If I could do things over, I would have found a way to keep my youngest daughter in this private Christian school. This school had been so good to her and to us—and she felt included at this school. I also feel, as I look back (and having learned more), that she might have fallen into the autism spectrum and attention deficit area. We have learned so much more about the wide range of autism over the years. Our daughter seemed to always fall into the lower average range, but she did learn the things that she really wanted to and was interested in, like getting her driver's license.

I loved being a mother and was involved in each of my children's classes, being a room mother and volunteering in different school activities. I was also involved in Sunday school and scouting. I would bake and decorate cut-out cakes and make special treats and favors for their classes. My husband wanted me to stay at home and not work, so I enjoyed all the time with my children, occasionally doing in-home child care to give my kids playmates and for a little extra money. I also enjoyed sewing some of my children's clothes.

I believe our children had a pretty good, normal life. They had pets and had all the necessities and many of the extras. They loved playing outside in their huge sandbox that their dad made for them, swinging on their tire swing, and riding their big wheels down our hill with the neighborhood kids. Our neighbors' kids also shared a homemade go-cart with our kids. We celebrated their birthdays with special decorated cakes, which I most often made and cut out and decorated! The kids had special birthday parties and always had very special Christmases. They were able to have many friends and special pets: fish, bunnies, a duck, cats, and dogs.

I loved my children very much and always wanted what was best for them. I will admit I was strict and old-fashioned, but I feel I most often tried to be fair. I also liked to have a clean and orderly home with routine, which I find is important to most of my children and grandchildren today. As I look back, though, I could have relaxed a little on some things. I had to implement the discipline, which was consequences and an occasional spanking once in a while but every day shared hugs and kisses with them to let them know I loved them. We would read almost every day or night and shared bedtime prayers and special time together.

Also as I look back, I was probably overly protective of all my children. I was the parent, not their best friend, when they were growing up. I was very surprised to see that some parents, even good parents and Christian parents, would allow underage drinking and also sleepovers with their boyfriends or girlfriends in their homes. I found that to be even more so when raising my granddaughter. These parents who were their kids' friends made it harder for us parents who were not. The computer and cell phone age has also made being involved as a parent very important. As my children have become adults and have children of their own, I hope they better understand why I chose to remain their parent during their years growing up. I truly hope that we have become friends over the years! I do have to admit that the teenage years were not my favorite years, though, as we were all very strong-willed in our home, which sometimes made things very interesting. You have to love your teens in order to sometimes like them and their attitudes—and the choices they sometimes make during those years.

From the time I became a mom—I loved it—and I took that job and responsibility very seriously, maybe too seriously. It was only when I became a mom that I began to realize how important Jesus needed to be in my life and in the lives of my children, as I raised them. So we had our children baptized and later confirmed. Back in the day we had to agree to our children being baptized and raised in the Catholic church since my husband was Catholic. When our first child Danielle was baptized, we weren't even able to be in the same room because there were so many babies being baptized at the time. My husband and I had to stand outside this small room to allow the sponsors to be in with the babies. This bothered me as this was a very special day for our baby girl, and we wanted to be close to her. So when our son was born, we chose to have him baptized privately so we could actually be a part of it. We went on to have our children attend my church for their Christian education, as there wasn't anything at the time for early education unless children attended the Catholic schools. My husband began attending my Protestant church so we could attend as a family. Later our youngest daughter was baptized in this church, as well as our grandchildren.

As I look back on those days, I don't think God would have really cared what church we were married in, or where our children attended for their early education. The main thing was that we were married and raising our children in a Christ centered church. My commitment to raise my children to know that there was a God who loved them was very important to me. I also wanted them to know Jesus as their personal Savior, falling in love with Him and being guided and directed by Him.

From the time my oldest child, Danielle, started Sunday school at the age of three, we would attend Sunday school and church every Sunday. I became a Sunday school teacher for twenty-plus years; actually, this was where I began to learn and understand who Jesus really was. I was very dedicated to growing in my faith and to teach my children that knowing and loving God was very important. Going to Sunday school and church was never an option in our home; it was always something that was expected of my children through high school, even though they bucked it many times. We prayed daily at meals and bedtime, hoping that would be a lifelong commitment to them. My two oldest children attended a weekly Awana group at one of the churches. Back in those days, we did not talk much about the personal relationship with Jesus, though, which we have learned is the most important part. I am disappointed that my adult children have not carried through with a lifelong commitment to being involved in a church of their own. Is it because of my making them attend too much Sunday school and church, some of the things that have happened at past churches we attended, or just the times we live in?

My dreams, hopes, and prayers are for each one of my adult children, grandchildren, and future great-grandchildren to build a strong personal relationship with their Lord and Savior, Jesus Christ, and pass it on to their family. I *TRUST* in God that through Him it will happen in His time! God can truly make a real difference in each one of our lives if we put Him and others first.

During my marriage and raising our children there were times that were rocky and scary. There was a time I was so scared that I might have a serious physical problem. My doctor was sending me to a larger hospital, as there was a spot on my neck that he had found on an X-ray. I prayed to God and promised Him that if everything turned out okay, I would never worry about finances and be anxious about things again. Anxiety ran rampant in my family, and I was starting to worry more about things. I had seen my mom deal with anxiety and obsessive worry and later on my sister and her children. I was so worried and concerned for what might be happening. As a young mom, having little children, I had to wait for a month—which seemed like a year—as I imagined the worst. What was it, and could it be cancer?

I was finally seen by a doctor and found out it was scar tissue from a broken vertebrae in my neck from a previous car accident when I was a teenager. (Jesus was also watching over me on the day of this accident—but I never realized that at the time). I look back on how I had scared and worried my paternal grandmother, who had to worry about me after I was brought to my grandparents' home after my accident out in our county. She was already dealing with cancer herself and was taking care of my grandpa, who also had cancer.

Our accident happened in a rural area on a cold winter day in December, two days before Christmas. There were four of us involved, and the other three were taken to the hospital from surrounding towns that had ambulances. I was the least seriously hurt, so I was taken by car to my grandparents' house and then my dad transported me back to my mom's house that night. I did not go to the hospital until the next morning where I found out I had a broken ankle, a broken collarbone, broken vertebrae in my back and neck, and a fractured skull. Needless to say, I spent that Christmas in the hospital. We were all so very lucky to be alive! The two-door car had slid on a patch of ice and rolled several times off of a high hill, jumping a culvert, landing us all in a cornfield—all being thrown out one car door, as the driver was pinned in on the other side.

Thank God that the news of my neck was not serious and for His calming me during this storm and relieving my anxieties and my worries. From that point on, I was starting to leave a lot of my worries and cares in the hands of God!

Another big "trust in God" moment happened when our children were three, eight, and twelve. My husband, Paul, had lost his job for a year and a half, and we had to endure a long, bitter strike in our town. A couple months into the strike, he was able to get minimal work, building tall grain buildings. He hated heights, but it was a job, and he needed to provide for his family. Since there was a strike, no one would hire him permanently. We now had to pay for our own family health insurance each month, with little income. At this time we had three young children and I was a stay-at-home mom. Before this, we were in the process of looking for a larger home, so that was put on hold.

I believe this was the very beginning of where I began to start really believing in a living God and trusting Him. It was amazing how we were able to get by with so very little during that time and were able to maintain our savings that we had put back for our larger home. We were able to pay our bills and lived okay during that time. Actually, I think our family was closer through this time as we had to get along and work together and trust that God would provide and take care of us. And He did! As I look back on this, I believe it even more today. I have learned that Jesus is our security and an anchor for our soul, as it says in Hebrews 6:19. We can have this hope—when we trust in God—to be able to live a peace-filled, joyful life, knowing God is our great hope!

The strike was very hard on my husband as he was a hard worker, and it was very important to him to take good care of his family. He had always done a very good job of that, working long hours. It seemed that most of the responsibility of raising our children fell onto me, which wasn't really uncommon during those years. My husband knew I would take good care of the kids, so he let me do most of the parenting. I was blessed that our children were very well behaved out in public and at school, and most often also at home. I wish my husband and I could have been closer as a couple and that we could have worked and parented together better, for our children's sake. That would be something I would do different today, if I were to go back.

My husband, Paul, didn't deal with stress very well, though, and would sometimes drink to relax and work through his stress. My husband wasn't an everyday drinker, but when he did drink, it would alter his personality, and he would get very angry—and

I was sometimes his target. There was mostly verbal and emotional abuse, which I found out later could be worse than the physical abuse. Only once was there physical abuse, and that was when we separated. After my husband would calm down after drinking, he would use silence to hurt me or go into a depression, and that could last for weeks. In working with a counselor later, I learned that stressful situations could possibly revert my husband back to hurtful times in his life, having lost three of his family members in such a short time during his younger years and also a physical eye injury in the service. Stressful situations could cause him to go back to those traumas in his life, as he may have not been able to move through and past them. I also learned through therapy and reading, that as a daughter of an alcoholic father, I could have seen my role as trying to fix my husband. I found out later that it is only God who can really heal people. We just need to let go and pray for them! We often need to be the ones who change the way we do things in order for things to turn out differently.

Later on as a teenager and adult, our son, Shannon, also had problems with alcohol and gave us some testy, concerning years, as he battled with depression and anxiety, while using alcohol as his medication. I found out later that a place he had worked as a teenager had allowed alcohol to be a big part of closing-time activities. Here I thought I was helping my son be responsible by having a job, and this was all going on. There were many times my son did not like me for taking a stand and holding him accountable. There was a period of time, where he left our home to live with his older sister for a while. As we have talked later, my husband and I wish we would have had a serious talk with our oldest daughter before she agreed to let her brother come stay with her, as he was avoiding dealing with what was going on.

When he was a young teenager, I had talked very openly with my son about the concerns of alcohol addiction, as it ran on both sides of my family and also with the alcohol problem his dad had. I wanted him to know he would have to be very careful when he would choose to drink, as he would be at high risk with all the alcohol addictions in our family. The males seemed to be more at risk in my family, as both my dad, Merle, and his grandfather were alcoholics, as well as a girl cousin on my dad's side. On my mom's side, there was her brother and also my brother who had some alcohol problems. Of course, kids don't think parents know anything, and he did not listen to me. Later on he told me that around sixteen or seventeen, he was not feeling as comfortable socially (in his younger years he was very outgoing and social) and that he was dealing with depression. So he chose alcohol for his own medication, although he was smart enough to know that it would only depress him more.

Going back to the time that my husband was on strike, I started to work part time in the evenings and weekends as a decorator consultant for a Christian decorating company. I would go into homes to help women decorate and help them to feel good about their home and themselves. They would have in-home decorating parties with their friends and earn gifts for their homes. I absolutely loved this job, although it was a very physical job, carrying a lot of merchandise in and out. I continued to work part-time in my own business for over twenty years. I was able to meet so many neat, wonderful people, and we had so much fun! I was also able to travel across the country as we would go to different conventions. The philosophy of this company was that God wanted women to feel good about themselves and know they are special and loved by Him. I would give the lady hosting the party a rose, letting them know that God loved them, and I appreciated and thanked them for being my hostess and inviting us all into her home. Later on, my youngest daughter, Heidi, would go with me as my helper to carry things in and out with me, and I would pay her a little to help.

I also co-owned a gift store for over thirteen years, and also loved that. My partner and I built our business on personal service to all of our customers. My granddaughter, Kynnedi, as a little girl, loved to help me in my store, designing her own baskets. She wanted to be able to work there someday, and when we were going to close the store, she was so upset. I've always made an effort to enjoy the things I was doing at the time and loved meeting new people and getting to know them. I remember a minister once saying, "Whatever work you do—do it as if you are doing it for the Lord."

As I look back over our fifty-four years of marriage, we have had many wonderful times, and we have also gone through some horrible times, as a couple. There were a couple of times, where we really struggled, and we separated for quite a period of time. Through those times, I relied on God to give me the strength and wisdom that I needed—as I could have never done this alone without Him. I took my marriage vows very seriously, and I would oftentimes go to His Word, the Bible, for His direction and guidance as to what I should do. Even though I didn't always have a clear sense of what I was supposed to do, I would find His comfort, wisdom, strength, and guidance to get me through the night and into the next day! God was my guiding light.

Chapter 3

A Mother's Worst Nightmare

Then came the most horrible nightmare that we would ever have to deal with—learning about the most horrific thing that happened to our youngest daughter! This was absolutely unbelievable to me—and still is today! Watching our youngest child, Heidi, struggle in school was bad enough, but then learning later of her sexual abuse was almost unbearable for me to grasp as her mom. This is the time that Jesus became my very best friend—as He often carried me through unbelievable times and long, sleepless nights. He was the only one who was always there for me and who I could always count on, no matter what! What I didn't know then was that this was only the very beginning of what was to be a very long journey of many, many years of struggles and heartaches for my daughter and the rest of us!

As I look back, I believe I tried to advocate for my daughter in school. She had a rough start when she first started school, and kindergarten was a not a good fit for her. Heidi and her teacher weren't a good match, and we saw her start to regress. She was going backwards for the first couple months of kindergarten, instead of forward, and she was starting to stutter and not able to repeat the things at school that she knew at home. I was seeing her teacher put her on the spot and put her down—even in front of me. I did speak up some to the principal at the time, but he stood up for his teacher. I began to see a whole different side of this principal with my youngest daughter, compared to the principal I saw with my older two children. From my viewpoint as a mom, this teacher was very cruel to my daughter. So my husband and I decided to move her, in the middle of her kindergarten year to a private Christian school. She did much better, and we were able to keep her there through the second grade. But then our oldest daughter, Danielle, was going to be starting college, and we didn't feel we would be able to afford both expenses. So we decided to move our younger daughter, Heidi, back to the public school where there were also extra resources for her.

Later on, it was hard to see Heidi struggle in other areas of her life. She felt like she never quite fit in. As she entered the teen years, we saw her making poor choices and having self-destructive behaviors. She would act out by stealing from neighbors and from us, her parents, also from her brother and sister—and even her grandmother who she dearly loved and who loved her so very much. We couldn't understand why she would do that. Later, as we found out more about her sexual abuse, we learned that this behavior sometimes is a part of that, as she had had her innocence stolen from her. It was almost unimaginable, as a mom, to think that this was all going on with my little girl, and we couldn't reach her or get through to her.

As our daughter Heidi grew older, into later middle school and high school, things only got worse! We began seeing more behaviors that were very disturbing, more stealing, lying, sneaking out, and cutting herself. I tried to understand her and get her all the help through counseling and therapy. For a while she was going twice a week to a psychologist out of town and a counselor in town. She was also in a sexual abuse support group that they had at the time in our city. Heidi seemed to do much better while in this group. As part of her group therapy, she was encouraged to go around in our immediate neighborhood to alert the parents of younger children of what had happened to her. She seemed empowered, like she felt better about herself. We were very proud of her for doing this, as it probably was very hard for her not to know if people would believe her or not. We were really encouraged that this would help her move forward to heal and feel better about herself. Heidi always seemed to do better with encouragement from us and others to stay on track. But we also found she would do well for a while and then regress. No matter how much we tried to stand with her, walking alongside her and getting help for her, nothing we said or did seemed to improve her self-esteem nor make any permanent changes for the long-term good. It was almost like she would self-sabotage when things were going well. I often wondered what our daughter was trying to tell us when she was stealing from family, neighbors, at school, and at church. Was she lashing out at God, me, and others for not protecting her from the abuse happening to her? Why was she cutting herself? When she left me notes to find, was she hoping I could figure things out? Over the years, as I have learned more about sexual abuse and human trafficking, at first perpetrators are very nice to children as they befriend them and begin to groom them. Then they often move on to threaten to harm their victims and their family and pets to keep them quiet. Was our daughter trying to protect us? Was she too afraid to tell? I had found many more details that I will not share that disturb and bother me greatly. This was a little girl, and some of the things I have read and heard would frighten any adult, let alone a little child!

My heart breaks for this little child that I loved and didn't seem to be able to help! How much of this had affected my daughter's learning, her mental health—and her whole life?

Our daughter had been diagnosed with conduct disorder and fundamental thought disorder, depression; also she showed signs of bipolar and personality disorder around fourteen, when she was hospitalized in our area. She was very impulsive, sneaky, and secretive, and had very risky behaviors, which continued to be a concern as she made poor choices of friends throughout her teen years. We had tried to get her into a behavioral hospital for a thirty-day program at seventeen to see if things could be turned around and she would improve, but we were denied the stay and found out later our insurance refused to pay for the program. Had I known this was the reason at the time, I would have totally bucked this and demanded our insurance pay for this, as we had good insurance through my husband's work. That day we had been sitting out at the hospital waiting to be admitted, finding out later they were just giving us the run around as to why they wouldn't be able to admit her. I had been on the phone for hours that morning, making all the arrangements before we had left our town. I was told exactly what to do when we got to this hospital which was about an hour and a half away. So when the hospital found out about our insurance's refusal to pay for this thirty-day program, they lied to us and made excuses why they couldn't admit our daughter. If we had been told the truth, we would have figured out a way to get our daughter the treatment she needed. We should have at least been granted a forty-eight-hour stay and the truth!

So very sad, as this could have maybe been the place that things could have seriously been addressed and changed! We also found out during this time that our daughter had been date raped, so we had yet one more thing added to the multiple traumas that our daughter had already gone through. I believe her behaviors were her way of trying to tell us all that things were not right with her, but she didn't have the words, and she was frightened by those who had threatened or hurt her. I found out in her writings years later that she had been threatened by the man who sexually abused her, saying that he would kill her and also threatened to harm or kill all her family. Oh my! How could a little girl deal with all of this? Why didn't she come to us and tell us, and why weren't we able to get her the help that she so desperately needed?

Having had watched my children very closely, living in this safe, middle-class neighborhood, made it so very hard for me to understand all that had happened to my daughter in this so-called "safe neighborhood." I questioned did this really happen? How could it have happened? For many years after finding out of my daughter's abuse, I couldn't trust anyone, and I didn't want to be friendly with any neighbors at all. That was an awful feeling not to know who to trust. Our daughter revealed later in therapy that the abuse started happening with a baby kitten when she was eight years old and lasted until she was eleven years old. But later on as we found more things out, I wonder if things could have even happened sooner—like when we first moved to this neighborhood—and have continued longer?

My husband had a very hard time in dealing with all that was going on and what he really wanted to do to the person that hurt his little girl. It had happened so close to home, and it was someone that he knew very well. One night, my husband was so outraged with everything that was going on and having been drinking, he physically assaulted me. That was the final straw for me! I knew he was hurting through all of this, but so was I, and I couldn't and wouldn't take any more! I filed a police report, we separated, and I filed for divorce and had every intension of carrying through! I too had a real hard time dealing with all of this, but I was not lashing out at him or my family. As I have gotten older and learned more, I feel I could have dealt with this situation much better. Gradually, God intervened to change my husband's heart, writing me a heartfelt letter, telling me he was sorry for what he did and asking for my forgiveness. After a period of about a year and a half, we were able to reunite. Although everything has not been perfect, God has gradually changed my husband into the person I always knew he could be.

Needless to say, the year that my husband and I were separated was an extremely rough year for my youngest daughter, Heidi, and for me. We were frightened by some things that were going on. Three obscene messages had been left on our answering machine, and I didn't know who they were from. Back in those days, there was no way to know, as names didn't show up on the phones. Were they left by the person who abused her? This person was close by in our neighborhood, and he knew pretty much what we were doing and whether we were home or away—and that my husband wasn't with us.

As I look back, I'm not really sure how we did make it or get through it all. As the poem "Footprints in the Sand" says, (in which the person questions why there were not two sets of footprints in the sand when they needed the Lord the most), "I don't understand when I needed you most you would leave me." The Lord replied, "My precious child, I love you and would never leave you. During times of trials and suffering, when you see only one set of footprints in the sand—it was then that I carried you." God must have carried me some, for I don't even know if I was really there myself. There was really no help for parents going through this. We had our daughter in a lot of counseling—and sometimes they would talk with us—but pretty much we were on our own to deal with all of this. There was an investigation and it came back "unfounded." Back in those days, sexual abuse was not addressed like it is today.

Thank God, we have looked at this issue and do much better at believing our children, instead of just the adults. We had our daughter in counseling for many years, trying to help her deal with all this, and we also don't know how this had affected her early school years, her self-worth, and her mental health. There was a time Heidi would not sleep in her bed, only on the floor in her room. What was she trying to tell us? I believe the sexual abuse hurt and destroyed so much of my daughter's life as a child and also contributed to a lot of the further destructive behavior in her later life as an adult.

Our daughter, Heidi, left our home on her eighteenth birthday and never returned to live in our home again (except for a couple months when she was married to her first husband). At this time we were beginning to see early signs of alcohol and drugs. She eventually quit school (she did later on get her GED) and chose to be with abusive boyfriends and run with people making bad choices. She was also supported by many enabling parents and adults with no expectations or rules. It was so very, very sad, as we watched our daughter become someone we didn't even know. She did the complete opposite of whatever we had taught her. She would hurt us—her parents, her siblings, and her grandmother—without it even seeming to bother her at all and eventually her own children. Was it intentional? Did she blame us, or mainly me, for not protecting her and keeping her safe? What was really going on?

The rebellious, destructive lifestyle she was leading was unbearable to watch and hear about. I would wake up during the night to a phone call and be so frightened for what might be happening to my daughter. I would also be fearful of getting a phone call or the doorbell ringing during the night to hear she was hurt or dead. I would go to my Bible and open it and read God's Words for the comfort I would find there. I would feel Jesus's loving arms around me when I would try to go back to sleep. I would pray—but oftentimes felt God wasn't listening—as we saw no changes.

I would often try to talk to my daughter and try to get her to look at what was happening, but she wouldn't listen, and nothing changed. She would lash out to us the most—me in particular. I could never understand how she would constantly run to her abusive boyfriends who would constantly beat on her and mistreat her, than to be able to stay safe within her family. As a little girl, my youngest daughter was so very close to our family and seemed to love us so much! How could she just detach from everyone and not be bothered by it? I could hardly believe it was the same person that I knew and raised.

This type of behavior went on for a couple years, and I would pray—and pray—and pray—for things to improve and she would see the light. These types of behaviors, I later learned, are very common in people involved with drugs and having mental illness. They are usually trying to escape the pain they are in. Often they have to go back through that pain in therapy; that is very hard for them to do, and they often run away to avoid it.

Did the sexual abuse lead to my daughter's mental illness—or was the mental illness there and made worse by it? I remember when Heidi was around nine years old, she mentioned, as she sat at the end of our counter during dinner, that this neighbor man had touched her ear. And she had acted out a couple times in the next couple years—which wasn't like her—but it didn't make sense to me or raise any alarm bells at the time. Touching one's ear wouldn't be considered sexual abuse, but my daughter must have felt uncomfortable about this, even though she couldn't express herself—and I didn't know enough about this to pick up on what she did say to us.

Today it does send red flags out, as I have learned so much more about how perpetrators begin to groom and set the stage to victimize children—first in little uncomfortable ways to see if they can get by with it without anyone telling on them! This man knew way too much about our family and our life; he had been in our home several times, even watching Heidi's cat when we took our family trip to Florida. I found out later in her writings that he had scared her by saying he was watching her and knew where she was all the time and where she slept, as he had been in her bedroom. My daughter had also filled in for her brother sometimes on his paper route, which made her easily accessible on those days for this man to make her feel uncomfortable and/or continue to groom or abuse her. Yet another occurrence in those younger years, which my daughter wrote about and which I found later, is so devastating to read and so personal that I will not share.

I found out later, when Heidi started high school that this man had been stalking her, as I actually caught him one morning when she was leaving for school, so I started to drive her to her bus stop. I had caught her earlier, taking a shortcut through a wooded area and had told her not to do that as she needed to stay on the main sidewalk coming home from the bus, but I did find her doing it again. Was she trying to avoid this man that I found stalking her later? Why didn't she just tell us?

Our oldest daughter, Danielle, later told me that she had caught this man following her and her boyfriend as they walked around our neighborhood in the evenings. She also thought he had peeked in her bedroom window at night, and even shared with me that one time when she was a junior in high school this man had given her a ride to the bus, as it had started to rain as she was walking down the hill to catch it. She said he had made her feel uncomfortable as he reached across her lap to open the car door for her. She said she didn't share this with me because she knew that she would never take a ride from him again. If I had been more educated about sexual abuse years ago more of these things might have been red flags to me. Please—if you ever get a gut feeling about someone, whether it is a family member, neighbor, or a friend, or if something doesn't seem quite right, keep a very close eye on the situation. Oftentimes things that happen are with a person that children know—oftentimes very well—and people they often trust. Tell your children to always come to you and tell you if anyone makes them feel uncomfortable or tells them not to tell anyone—no matter if they know this person well or what this person would say to threaten them or their family. Let them know that you will always listen and believe them and that you can be the one to help them. If you have young children, get as educated as you can! Take the "Darkness to Light" two-hour child sexual abuse training. I wish I would have had some of these things available back in the day when my little girl was growing up. Those days we talked about stranger danger, but over the years we have learned that most often, the serious dangers lurk with the people very close to us whom we know and trust.

Thank God I didn't know what would lie ahead—and that this was just the beginning of a very long painful road for my daughter and for us as her parents and eventually for her future children.

Chapter 4

Our Youngest Daughter and Her Children!

After my youngest daughter, Heidi, left our home, I had many sleepless nights and hours of tears and heartaches. Jesus continued to become my best friend more and more during this time. He was the one who carried me through these unbelievable times and long sleepless nights. I would hear of my daughter's boyfriend abusing her, but could do nothing. I remember one very cold winter night, I received a phone call, and on the other end of the line was someone saying my daughter had been beaten up and was lying on someone's doorstep. What was I to do? Back then there was no caller ID. I didn't know where she was. Would she freeze to death? This broke my heart. I would again go to the Bible to find some of God's comforting words to calm me and eventually be able to go back to sleep for a little while.

My daughter's first boyfriend was very abusive, and they lived with his mother who had also been abused and very mentally unstable so that situation was very unhealthy. I tried to go to their apartment, which was very messy and dirty to try to talk to my daughter but got nowhere with her. There was one time that we heard that my daughter had gone to work with bruises and was asked how she had gotten them, and she blamed her dad instead of her boyfriend. We had not even been with her, so we knew we had to be very careful if we were to be around her, as she oftentimes would lie to cover for her boyfriends. I had come to the point I could not trust my daughter—and that is a very sad place to be as a mom.

We would go for months not hearing anything from our daughter. We tried to think that no news was good news. Then we received word that Heidi left the state and traveled to Mississippi with her newest boyfriend, James. Our daughter would go on to have a history of having a new man right after leaving another one—or maybe even before she would leave the previous one.

Months later, we heard from our daughter that she was pregnant, and we were going to be grandparents. While we were excited about becoming grandparents and that this might be the permanent change we so wanted, we also were very concerned about a little one being involved in the middle of our daughter's very unstable, troubled life. We later found out that her boyfriend had our daughter working a couple of jobs, while living in a tent, as the boyfriend would lie around doing nothing.

As I worried about my daughter, Heidi, and her being able to have a successful pregnancy, I felt she would need the help and support of her family. I encouraged our daughter to come back closer to home so that we could maybe help her have a healthy pregnancy and baby—and to be there to help her to get some of the things that she would need for her baby. So when my daughter did ask for our help to come home, we said we were willing to help her, although we did not really want to encourage a relationship with this boyfriend. We were willing to pay for our daughter to fly home, but not for the boyfriend.

Of course my daughter's condition was that we would fly both her and her boyfriend home, or she would not come. So guess what we did?

Yes, we paid for two plane tickets! I often wonder if my daughter would have come home by herself if we would have absolutely refused to buy her boyfriend a plane ticket home. Looking back, I very much regret bringing him back, but I also realize that our daughter probably wouldn't have come back then either. Our daughter had originally wanted us to come to Mississippi to be a part of their wedding, but we felt it would be better that they would come back up to our town. We were here, also her extended family was here, and I felt that she might need us all for emotional and probably financial support.

So our daughter, Heidi, and her boyfriend came back to our town and were married on Christmas Eve in a very small private wedding in a blizzard snowstorm on top of a steep church hill. So the already small private wedding turned into even a smaller gathering, as most of the people could not get there. Under the circumstances, it was probably a blessing! I would like to say much more, but I won't. Shortly after their wedding we received this note:

Dear Mom and Dad,

Thank you so much for everything you guys have done for us. Thank you for sending us home for Christmas and setting everything up for our wedding. I know it was such short notice, but everything turned out great. The wedding was so beautiful. Thank you both for walking me down the aisle. I will never ever forget that day. Thank you so much.

Love you always, Heidi and James

Heidi, and her new husband, James, who you can imagine I really didn't care for, lived with us for a couple of months in our home. I really tried my best to find the good in him and to give him a chance to prove himself, as he had not had much of a life himself. I'm sure him not having much stability in his life contributed greatly to the person he was. He did quickly find a job at a fast food restaurant but really didn't want to work, so he lost that job in a few days and made excuses as to why he didn't want to work those kinds of jobs. James really didn't get it that he was very lucky to even get a job, and he should have been happy to work and continue to look for something different that would be a better fit for him.

My husband and I helped our daughter and her husband to find a really cute apartment in a decent part of our city. I had to sign the lease and be responsible, as they had no credit—or bad credit. We were able to round up furniture from different places and also baby furniture. I, of course, wanted my first grandchild to have decent furniture, so we bought everything a baby needs pretty much new. Everything was set up so nice for them in this apartment!

This was a note we received from our daughter, shortly after her and her husband were settled in their apartment.

Dear Mom and Dad,

Thank you so much for everything you guys have done, for letting us have the chairs and table. Thank you so much for getting the beautiful table and the bed. We like it a lot. Thanks for letting us stay up there at the house until we got into the apartment. The place looks really beautiful. I will never forget what all you guys have done for us. Thank you so much.

Love you guys a lot,
Heidi

Things seemed to be going okay for a few months and our adorable little five-pound baby granddaughter, Kynnedi, was born! She was perfect! Of course, I might have been just a little bit biased! It wasn't very long, though, until the concern and worry began for my granddaughter's safety! First off, I was so embarrassed to see everyone under the sun show up at the hospital the night she was born, and then to have to see my little precious baby granddaughter riding home in a rundown beater car. This was not my idea of what I would have wanted for my first grandchild! Would it have been yours?

In just a few weeks, things began to fall apart with drugs and different characters hanging out around their place. Actually, evidence was there when our little granddaughter came home from the hospital, as I had found some evidence of drugs at the apartment. Also, on that day she was brought home, she was greeted by a cat that jumped on her in her infant seat, and they were not supposed to have a cat, according to their lease. Of course, rules were never that important to follow for my daughter, Heidi, and her husbands, boyfriends, and friends. I had helped them to get this apartment, and my name was on their lease—and it stated no cats—so I was concerned. I said "I could just take the cat with me," and James, my granddaughter's dad, got upset with me and the cops were called. It's kind of funny today, but I was very upset and bothered by this and so embarrassed at the time!

At six weeks old, I witnessed my little granddaughter, Kynnedi, swinging by her little lonesome in the living room, when I stopped by one time. Her dad was entertaining his friends, girls and guys, in the next room. I'm guessing they were doing some drugs, as there was a blanket covering the doorway. My daughter, Heidi, was at work at the time. I, of course, asked to take my granddaughter for a while, and her dad didn't care. So I grabbed this precious little bundle, and took her home with me for a while, so I knew she was safe. I would take my granddaughter as often as I could in order to try to keep her safe!

It wasn't long before my daughter Heidi, and her husband James, moved out of this apartment and shortly after that, they also separated. As I later tried to find answers to suspicions I had of different things, especially drugs, one day I visited some of the neighbors in that neighborhood to see if they had concerns about any drug activity or had seen anything. Of course, like I suspected, there were a couple of neighbors who gave me quite a lot of information about the many people they saw come and go, and the late-night activity at my daughter's house. Also, my daughter and her husband broke back in to this apartment to retrieve things left in the basement. The landlord could have pressed charges, but chose not to.

My little granddaughter, Kynnedi, was about six months old at the time when this was all happening. One night, my daughter came to pick up her daughter, as I had been watching her. I noticed that she had this spare tire lying up against the back seat of her car, and it wasn't secured in any way. They would be traveling on the highway for a bit to get to where they lived in another state. The tire was right next to where my granddaughter sat in her car seat. She had this old beater car, which had been having flat tires, and I was so concerned that if she would have to stop suddenly that this tire would roll over on my granddaughter and hurt or even kill her. I tried to talk with my daughter, Heidi, about how unsafe this was for her daughter, and I asked if my granddaughter could just stay the night with us. Of course, my daughter refused to let her stay because I had addressed safety concerns. I continued to just keep hold of my granddaughter, Kynnedi, and my daughter called the cops on me! Of course, I had no right to keep my granddaughter, and I had to let her go with my daughter, but I was very surprised that the officer did not mention anything about the safety of my granddaughter with this tire sitting beside her.

Shortly after the move to another state, my daughter was seen walking alone at night on a major highway. She seemed to have no fear! I wasn't sure where my daughter and my granddaughter were living but soon found out. They were now living across the river, in a small river town with a new boyfriend that she had met. I was continuing to see a very disturbing pattern of scary things going on in my daughter's life!

I soon became very concerned of the unclean and unsafe living conditions that my daughter and her new boyfriend were living in. One time in February, I went to pick up my daughter and my then nine-month-old granddaughter Kynnedi, as she had been so very sick and running a high temperature. My daughter was in need of a ride to take her to the doctor. I walked into this trailer where I was greeted by the new boyfriend, Chance, who I hadn't met yet, sitting in his boxer shorts watching a big screen TV while the floor was covered with dog and cat feces. He directed me to the back bedroom where my granddaughter and daughter were. Here was my little granddaughter, Kynnedi, sick and lying in her crib that was still at the highest level as for a newborn (this was after my husband had asked my daughter if she had lowered the crib multiple times—and she said yes she had. He had even offered to come and do it.)

My little granddaughter had only a diaper on, and next to her bed was the bed my daughter and her boyfriend shared with no sheets and burn holes on the mattress. I asked my daughter if she had clothes to put on my granddaughter and she said, "Somewhere," as she looked among the clothes strewn all over on the floor among the feces. We finally found something and were off to the doctor's office. I'm sure you can imagine that I was not too happy with my daughter and her lack of real concern for her own daughter, but I tried to keep my cool as best I could, which wasn't easy to do! I also found out later in writings that my little granddaughter had been left all alone in this trailer for about an hour one night, as her mom and this boyfriend had to run an errand out of town. What if this little baby had choked or fallen out of bed—or if there had been a fire? Thank God, he was watching over this little one from very little on! There was a later founded report on this. There was some evidence, which I later found in my daughter's writings, that this had bothered her as she looked back on it.

I also remember a time when my granddaughter was only one, and she went for a visit with her biological dad, James, and the cops were called on him for some reason (he had a history of being in trouble with the law). My daughter was at work and luckily my sister-in-law, Diane, had heard this on the scanner and told me. I was able to go and pick up my granddaughter. As I'm putting my little granddaughter in her car seat, her dad was handcuffed and being put in the police car. If I wouldn't have been there to get my granddaughter, DHS would have been called, and she would have had to go with a stranger.

Another time, my granddaughter, Kynnedi, had gone with her dad, James, for a week in another small town about forty-five minutes away. She was about a year and a half then. She had a little cold when she left, so I was concerned about her and had asked my daughter, after a few days that she was gone, if she had talked to Kynnedi's dad to see how she was doing. My daughter said "No," that she had not talked to him. I said, "Are you not concerned how she is doing and when do you plan on getting her back? And she said "I don't know, we never set anything up for her to be returned." My daughter had a way of not really being much into concerns for her daughter. It was more about her doing the things she wanted to do. My daughter was twenty-three but was very irresponsible and immature at that age.

This was happening around Christmas time, and I was working full time at my store. I was thinking about my little granddaughter a lot and that she certainly could not take care of herself—and that we had a couple of very immature, unconnected, and seemingly very unconcerned parents. So I took it upon myself, after a week, to call up to this town's police station to see if they would do a welfare check on my granddaughter. I was lucky and did know the motel they were staying at. Of course, there were only a couple of motels in this smaller town. I was explaining my concern to the police officer on the phone. The police officer was not very friendly and felt that they didn't really have the time to do this and that I was just over concerned and overreacting. So I then got the number of the person in charge of the motel and called her to see if she had seen my little granddaughter with her dad at all. She said she had seen the dad—but not with a baby.

So *now* I am extremely concerned. So, you guessed it, I called back up to the police department, pretty much demanding they do the welfare check on my granddaughter! So they did, and in short time were calling me back at work. They said they had originally went to the motel and thought they saw someone peek out from the curtains but could get no one to answer the door. They then had to get the manager to let them enter, and when they did and saw a photo of my granddaughter's dad, they immediately went to his sister's house in the same town and told her that her brother had an hour to get my granddaughter back to her mother, or they would be putting out a warrant for his arrest. The police then called me to let me know that if she was not back to our town in one hour to let them know and what they would be planning on doing.

Unknown to me at the time, although I was very concerned about this dad, my granddaughter's father, James because he had been, and probably still was, involved with drugs, I was not aware that there were other concerns and eventually charges against him in this area. Later he did go to prison for the sexual abuse of two minor girls. This town, as I sometimes drive by it, has haunting memories for me; this is where it all kind of began for my precious little granddaughter. The craziness—the games—and the lies! Could anything have happened to her here? Had she been left all alone at her age?

During these months, both parents played games with my granddaughter back and forth. They would blame each other for things and basically only be thinking about themselves and what they wanted to do. My granddaughter, Kynnedi, had head lice twice, and both parents had been treating her with harsh, over-the-counter lice treatment. This treatment was not recommended to be used on young children under two years old, and my granddaughter was a little over one. I took my granddaughter a couple times, for a week at a time, to give her the home remedy—mayonnaise treatment—but neither parent cleaned up their houses and took this very seriously to remedy the problem. I have pictures of my little granddaughter at fourteen months, having her mayonnaise treatment with a plastic bag and towel wrapped around her head. We laugh today at the photo, but it certainly was not very funny then!

My husband and I did have to hire a lawyer to help my daughter, Heidi, get a divorce from my granddaughter's dad, James, in order to have any say over how often and long he could have her for visits and also to be able to put some safety issues in place when she would be with him. We were hoping that our daughter would take more responsibility after the divorce, but I am sorry to say, we continued to see that marriage, boundaries, and rules didn't really seem to make much of a difference to our daughter or to any of her friends!

So, a few months later, our daughter was pregnant with her second child by her new boyfriend, Chance. They had wanted to have another child, and they had moved to another trailer in this same trailer park, which was very run down. In the bedroom, where my granddaughter Kynnedi slept, there were exposed wires that no one seemed too concerned about, not even the landlord. Again we were dealing with cat feces and total disaster mess! Filth and clothing were scattered throughout this trailer with my granddaughter's clothing mixed in!

Our daughter and her second husband were married in a small private church ceremony at the church where she had been married before. They wanted something bigger, but we refused to pay for anything more than a simple wedding and family dinner at our home. So again we were trying to be supportive of them for the children's sake—not really understanding their irresponsible behavior of choosing to have more children when they could barely take care of themselves. Of course, you always love your children and realize that your grandchildren are caught up in the middle of this—and you dearly love and care about them and their welfare.

Our first grandson, Brady, was born nine weeks premature, weighing four pounds and just barely alive. He was quickly air-lifted to a larger major hospital an hour and a half away in the middle of the night because he was in such bad shape and at very high risk. After some time in the hospital, our grandson did come home on oxygen with major safety and health risks. As we had seen some bad choices and some neglectful situations made by these parents in the past, all four of us grand-parents were so worried for our grandson's health and safety. We decided to try to sit down and have a very serious talk with the parents and help them to understand the great risks and health problems this little boy was facing. We were hoping to get them to understand that it was crucial for him to be in a clean environment and have the best of care. We were hoping to help them have a fresh start!

So at first, it seemed like they were really on board with this idea. We bought a house to rent to them; eventually they could have owned it in time. The two dads bought a car for Chance to drive to work and gave it to them as a gift. Also with help, a job was found for our grandson's dad. Things went pretty well for a few months, but at best their parenting was minimal. However, it was much better than it had been. I would sometimes stop by the house to drop off my granddaughter after picking her up from preschool to find my little grandson, Brady, a little over a year old, sitting alone in the kitchen in his high chair eating cold spaghetti, while both of his parents were in the living room, watching TV. I chose to pick my battles as to when to say things, as it never took too much to set them off.

These adult parents were decent to us grandparents and seemed to appreciate our help in getting them off to a fresh new start! My husband and I paid for our granddaughter to attend two years of preschool, and we would all help with transportation. Our granddaughter, Kynnedi, did very well at preschool. Our grandson, Brady's, paternal grandparents were so wonderful and caring to both our grandson and also to our granddaughter. If ever a couple and family could have made it, this is where it could have, and should have, happened!

These parents were off to a good fresh start; they had a cute little house that they were renting from us, with the opportunity to own it over time. If they were responsible, all of their payments would have gone toward ownership of this house. We grandparents helped out with getting clothing and necessities for the kids and helping out with babysitting, as needed. We spent a lot of time uplifting and encouraging these parents! They had their own car, and also my grandson's dad had a good job at a local plant (which he had worked at a couple other times and had not continued to keep). His dad had helped to get him this job again—for the third time—as his dad was a foreman there.

But—

It wasn't very long before things were again falling apart, and our daughter and her second husband were no longer together. So instead of our daughter staying in the house with her children, which eventually would have been hers to own, she was off again with our two little grandchildren with a much older man this time—who rode a bike! She had been seeing this man, sneaking him in after her husband would leave for work in the early morning, and now the kids were off to living in three different places. The first place was an upstairs, all-male apartment, with a communal bathroom that everyone shared, and the kids did not have beds. I was so frustrated and very worried and afraid for the safety of these two little ones. I was so very upset with my daughter that she would not listen to anyone, especially any of us who wanted to see her and her kids have stability! But this was only the start of what was yet to come.

There were some very scary times in these months and years to come. There were a couple of months that our granddaughter was kept from us as there was suspicion of physical abuse of our granddaughter, Kynnedi, and grandson, Brady. My daughter and her boyfriend, Nathan, were being investigated. We were not really aware of all the circumstances surrounding this. We did know that we had seen some physical marks and bruises on both their bodies that the kids and my daughter and her boyfriend told different stories about. Our granddaughter came once with a black eye and marks on her side, with concerns of how they happened. Sometimes my daughter and Nathan hadn't even noticed injuries on the children and said they had no clue how the kids would have gotten those marks, or the different stories didn't quite fit. I found out later, through reports, that there had been a couple of investigations with some services put in place to help out. I also found out later, in reports, that my granddaughter had been accused of telling Pinocchio lies. I was so upset to think that she was the one accused of lying by the worker—when in fact it was probably her mother and/or boyfriend doing the lying. Within the next three years, there were another couple of moves, and two more baby boys were born. Shortly after baby Michael was born, our daughter failed to show up at her five-year-old daughter's dance recital, and we found out later she had spent the day with her newer boyfriend who lived next door. At the time, we were not aware of this. Then another year later, little baby boy, Zachery, was born a couple months early. So now we have four grandchildren, six years old and under!

My heart was breaking for all the concerns and worry I had. What would become of all of this? How could these four little children survive and be safe? How could my daughter ever take care of these four children under six years old? This would be a handful for any mom—even with fully being on board and giving it your all and consistently being with a responsible partner. My worries and concerns for these little children continued to grow as these children were so little and not able to fend for themselves or keep themselves safe. They really had no one to help them but us! As you could guess, my relationship with my daughter continued to get worse, as she continued to make bad choices. I would try to seriously talk with her, and she would go from "Yes, Mom" to "Get the hell out of my house."

I prayed and begged God. I reached out in our community to see if help could be given but was told the situation was not bad enough. So, I just continued to cry, worry, and pray for their protection! I had a high official in my city call me a crazy grandma, not directly to my face, but to someone else I knew. I've even called him on it; of course, he denied it. Maybe, as I look back, I could have been close to losing it. I was so very worried for these babies and didn't know what else to do to help them. As we continued to see very scary uncertain things going on and fearful for what might happen to our grandchildren, we decided to take out life insurance on my daughter and her children as we knew that we would be the ones responsible if ever anything, God forbid, would happen to one or all of them. My greatest fear was that these children would all end up dead if things did not change!

Chapter 5

My Daughter and Her Children— The Scariest Year Ever

When I thought things couldn't get any worse, the scariest year ever began! The older man, Nathan, the father of the two youngest boys, was eventually out—as my daughter had found "the one" as she had told me. For a short period of time, my daughter lived with her kids in their van, and then with her newest boyfriend, Lyle, in his mom's house in another state. That was until she could manage to get the older boyfriend out and be able to move back into her apartment. I did do some investigating about this newer man and found out that he had a history of sexual abuse of a minor. My little granddaughter would say to me that her mommy and this boyfriend were spanking her little brother Brady when he cried. She said, "Mommy's boyfriend spanks Brady when he is naughty." This little boy was not even four.

This boyfriend from hell, with all his tattoos and body piercings covering his skinny body, said later, in a report, that he had done meth before he met up with my daughter. Do you think I believed he stopped? Now my four little grandchildren (six and under) were living in a household with him—and with many other adult men and women who had lost custody of their own children. These people were staying in the house with my grandchildren—sometimes watching them while my daughter, Heidi, would work during the night, delivering papers.

There was a lot of suspicious drug activity going on at this house, with many people coming and going. It was common, when I would stop by, that five to twelve different people—both female and male—would be there lying on the floor sleeping, all over the house. I also feel my daughter, Heidi, was being taken advantage of by many of these characters, as I feel the money that was coming in to help her children was supporting a lot of these adults. When I would stop by for a short time, there would be guys stopping by and going into the front bedroom. I would see many different cars, some from out of the area, when I would pull up. I again would try to talk to my daughter about my concerns, but she would say, "My friends are fine and are good to my kids."

My little granddaughter, Kynnedi, once shared with me that Lyle dyed her bunny orange at Halloween, and she was so sad and bothered by that. She also said, "I tell Mama baby Zachery is crying, and Mommy just sits there." I also saw baby Zachery swinging at five months old, all wrapped up papoose style so he couldn't move. My grandson, Brady, would say that Lyle hits and hurts him, and my granddaughter would say that he leaves a rash on Brady when he spanks him. Kynnedi also said that her mom and her two boyfriends and a girlfriend spank her brother, Brady.

You see my granddaughter was wise and mature, way beyond her little years. My concerns and worries continued to grow, as the adults were sleeping all over the place until late in the morning or early afternoon. The children were not being properly cared for as they were kept in their beds or rooms most of the day and night. The home was kept dark with hopes of the babies staying asleep, as they were on the main floor among all these adults as they slept. When the adults were awake, these babies were subjected to very loud music and fighting. My little granddaughter, Kynnedi, was the little mommy to her three little brothers, trying to get them something to eat and drink, walking over people laying around the house while she was getting yelled at. My granddaughter was being a parent to her three little brothers (what they call being *parentified*) at six years old. I was very concerned about drugs being a big part of this household—and one Saturday morning, when I stopped by, I believe I was witnessing a meth lab being dismantled, as there were a couple of trucks there and some guys were taking things out of the garage in back. I had questioned a couple of neighbors in the area, who also were very suspicious of drug activity.

We also found out these adults would take the kids' blankets to use at night, leaving them without. So our family rounded up blankets to bring down to the house so that they would let the children have their blankets to keep warm. My granddaughter, Kynnedi, was so very scared of the one man—her Mom's most recent boyfriend, Lyle, who lived there—as he had broken in the bathroom door while my granddaughter was in the tub, and scared her badly.

I tried to prepare my granddaughter as to what to do if that would ever happen again—as I was so very worried and scared to what could possibly happen to this adorable little girl, as she was so vulnerable in this household of many men. My first thought was to tell my granddaughter to quickly get out of the tub and the bathroom but later decided she probably might be safer to just be still and not draw any attention to herself, as I wasn't sure what this person might do to her. Where was my daughter, her mother, at? Why was she not in the bathroom, watching my granddaughter while she was bathing anyway? Was she so depressed—high on drugs—being physically abused—or all three? What was going on, and how could these little children continue to survive and go on like this without some serious intervention?

My little four-year-old grandson, Brady, was most often barricaded up in his room with two baby gates and bars on his window, and we found out later that the child-protective department was aware of this. There was nothing on his walls, no toys and no blankets. It was heartbreaking, as I didn't know what more I could do to help him or all of them.

I later found out that my six-year-old granddaughter, Kynnedi, and my four-year-old grandson, Brady, had missed many days of school and that my daughter, Heidi, was not getting out of bed to get them ready for school. I also found out later that my daughter had not put either of us local grandparents on for an emergency call at the kid's school. She put her boyfriend Lyle's mom's phone number as the emergency number, but she lived farther away. This was so that no one who really cared would know or be suspicious of anything going on.

Many times, at the house, they weren't answering the phone or the door. I had tried to alert the school, the doctor's office, and a couple times I did call the Department of Human Services and also made a call to the County Attorney's office to share my concerns. We had four little children that were in a house with many sketchy adults with great suspicion of drugs going in and out of there—and my four little grandchildren were neglected and at serious risk of harm. Why was no one doing more? I was told it wasn't bad enough to do anything yet—that I had the best of the worst—and it had to get worse before anyone would do anything! I did find out later that the school made phone calls to the house. Of course, the parents didn't answer. I asked what they did then and was told after the children were missing for a couple days, they would go to the house to do a welfare check—and of course the parents just didn't answer the door. So I learned that my four little grandchildren were pretty much on their own, with no one really knowing how they were doing!

How my four grandkids made it out of this alive is an absolute miracle! What I found out later was that my prayers were being answered. It was God's protection and His watching over my grandchildren that kept them safe—as none of the adults in the house were really caring for them or watching them. There were a couple of years that I just had to pray and trust God to watch over and protect these precious little ones. It wasn't easy though. Many times I would pray and tell God I trusted Him and then try to do more myself to help if I could. I had to be very careful, as I stopped by the apartment every couple days, that I didn't do anything to permanently be kept out. If no one else could do anything for my grandchildren, then I had to make sure I could get into this house to check on them and to make sure they were safe and alive.

When I would stop by, I usually only stayed about fifteen or twenty minutes, as I probably would have gotten myself in trouble, and someone might be going to jail—and it would probably have been me! That would have been okay, if I would have been guaranteed help for my grandchildren. One time when I stopped by early in the afternoon to find about fifteen men and woman sleeping all over and the kids still in their beds, I made the comment "Is there anyone in this house who thinks that maybe this situation isn't normal?" Whoa! That brought the tattoo-covered boyfriend flying out of the front bedroom, and he became very much upfront and personal to me, right in my face. I was just waiting for him to hit me as I knew if he did, I would be filing charges! But he lucked out, and one of his friends jumped up off the floor and pulled him away from me.

My two little grandsons, Michael and Zachery, were under two years old and were confined to their crib or pack and play the majority of the day and night. Baby Zachery slept in a pack and play with a sleeping bag and pillow at five months old, and he was so overweight and barely able to lift himself up. I was so worried he would smother to death. He was often not dressed and had to nurture himself by rocking back and forth and banging his head; he continues to do that today into his teen years. The little ones were hardly ever able to get out on the floor to be able to learn to crawl and walk. They were both very delayed in their development. Whenever I would stop by the house to check on the kids, they were often in their beds or bedrooms.

When Zachery was three months old, he had RSV and was taken by ambulance during a blizzard to a hospital out of town. He was supposed to be taken by helicopter, but the weather was too bad for the helicopter to come. Neither one of his parents seemed too concerned at all of the seriousness of his illness; they said "It's just RSV." The doctors were very concerned and didn't think he was going to make it—but after about ten days in the hospital, he was better and able to go home.

I also found out later that my four-year-old grandson, Brady, would be dropped off by the bus from preschool and the scary tattoo boyfriend, Lyle—who abused him—told him to get his f***** butt off the bus. Oh my, how did something not get done to address this as there were people who knew what was going on but had been told not to tell me—or I guess anyone else that maybe could have done something about it! I had been told it wasn't bad enough and that it had to get worse before anyone could intervene and anything could be done! WHAT? Wasn't this pretty bad and scary for my grandson—and these kids? If my grandson was being talked to like this in public—how was he being treated in the privacy of this home? The school knew this was going on—and did no more with this?

As a Grandma I'm thinking how much worse can it get? Will they all end up dead? If I would have known this was going on with my grandson, I would have been waiting for my grandson to get off that bus with my video camera ready and would have demanded *action* be taken by somebody—and I would have been marching on the street with signs for protecting my grandkids and demanding better care and *help* for them! I was already a wreck with what I already knew—and this would have been the final straw. I had been praying and begging for help, as I knew my grandchildren were being neglected and not being cared for properly! This little boy, who had ADHD, was acting like a wild animal at preschool and at his Christmas program. Why wouldn't he be when he had to live like a caged animal in this crazy, scary environment, among these people who were hurting him?

One time I stopped by my daughter's house to get my granddaughter, Kynnedi, some extra clothes, as she had spent the night with us. I walked into her bedroom, and there was a couple sleeping in her bed. I was so very upset and distraught. Even her very own bedroom was not her safe space. She had one man walk in on her while she was in the bathtub—and another couple sleeping in her bed. What if she wouldn't have been with me and she had been there sleeping in her bed and this would have happened?

I fell apart that Sunday because I didn't know what more I could do to help my little grandchildren. I did try to reach out to talk with someone about my concerns. One police officer was so kind and listened but said he didn't think anything would be done. He suggested I talk with my daughter about this, which I tried to do a couple days later when I had calmed down. My daughter just said, "You can just take her bed back." You see, we had given this twin bed to our granddaughter to sleep in, as it had been her mom's bed. My daughter totally missed the safety risks for her daughter; she was just mad because I had said something to her about her daughter's safety at six, asking if this could be her own private space with no others allowed in there but my daughter (her mother) and her little brothers. You see when our daughter, Heidi, needed something from us, she loved us—but watch out! If we ever voiced our concerns, we could go to hell!

Later my granddaughter said in a report that many people slept in her bed, and she would come home from school and all the adults were sleeping. My granddaughter had also reported that she is afraid of the people in her house and that there were a lot of them. Also she wrote that the people were putting bottles in the babies' cribs before they go to sleep at night, so they don't have to get up in the morning to feed them. What? Why would this have to continue before something was done to change this situation for these little ones?

With what had already happened to Heidi in her past, why wouldn't she be over the top in protecting her little girl? Why was she not understanding and getting it? Why was she trusting all her friends and thinking they were treating her children well? I did find out that there was one woman who often would stop by who really did care about these children and would sometimes watch them at her house. I'm very thankful for that. I learned later that oftentimes women who have been sexually abused don't set very good boundaries for themselves or for their children. Also, a woman who has been sexually abused will oftentimes be promiscuous. Their thinking really doesn't make sense to me, but I guess they don't feel very good about themselves.

This adorable blonde, blue-eyed, six-year-old girl was in among so many men, and my daughter didn't seemed concerned, or to really get it. I tried to educate my granddaughter, Kynnedi, in the best way I could to try to protect her. I read a book to her, recommended by professionals, *A Very Touching Book for Little People and for Big People* by Jan Hindman, to try and keep her safe in this scary environment she was in. I would have never read this to a six-year-old if this had not been a very dangerous situation. I felt I had to do whatever I could to try to protect her.

I would often stop by the house to see my grandchildren and check to make sure they were all okay. As you can imagine, my relationship with my daughter continued to decline as she made poor choices of friends and was not recognizing the safety measures she needed to make for her children. My grandson, Brady, and my granddaughter, Kynnedi, would cry and cling to me when I would get ready to leave their house. One time I had to push my granddaughter back in the house, as my granddaughter was crying and clinging to me and screaming, "Grandma, Grandma," as she would open the door after me and her mom would grab her and pull her back in while she would be kicking and screaming. I can't tell you how hard it was for me to leave those children alone in that mess. I feel very bad now, but I couldn't and didn't get too attached to the two little babies, Michael and Zachery, as I felt my heart being ripped out of my chest with the two oldest—and I could barely handle that. I knew whatever I did to help the oldest two children would also help the babies. But I was at my wits end to know what to do to help them anymore.

We found out later that our granddaughter had told an investigator that she was fearful of the boyfriend, Lyle, as he was yelling and hitting her little brother Brady. Later we found out there was a founded report on the one incident. She said she would try to wake up her mom in the morning so she and Brady could go to school but often couldn't. We found out in a report later that the kids had missed a lot of school; our granddaughter had missed fourteen days and our grandson missed thirty days of early learning in four months. There had also been many no shows to Comprehensive Rehab appointments for our grandson. I would often feel relieved when the school week came, thinking the two older kids were in school, to only find out they often weren't. Also, Kynnedi said she would go home after being with us, and her mom would ask her a bunch of questions about what she had said to me. Kynnedi had told this person that her mother had told her not to tell, but she told this worker that she did tell her grandma anyway because she knew her grandma could help her.

My daughter was quick to let people into her house and around her very vulnerable children. She would have a new guy lined up before she left the last one—and he was always "the one"—most often more dangerous and scarier than the last one. Toward the very end, my daughter had the scary tattoo guy, Lyle, and the next very abusive guy, Kevin, in the same house among her children, and they would often fight, so the kids were around a lot of domestic violence. Yes, that's right—two boyfriends in the same house! I still to this day can't understand why my daughter would have not been so very careful with her children after what had happened to her!

I continued to have my granddaughter stay with me as often as I could—and sometimes also her four-year-old brother—or give his dad a call to come get him when I stopped by and was very concerned. One time, my granddaughter said to me that her brother, Brady, was really lucky today because he is at his other grandparents today, and they live far away. When my granddaughter, Kynnedi, would spend the night at our house and I would be driving her to school the next morning, she would start to cry and not want me to leave her. I would go to drop her off at school and would tell her I would see her in a few days—and she would scream and cling to me as I would walk her into school. Her kindergarten teacher would witness this also. When I would voice my concerns about many of these things to others, I would be told that this behavior often happens with grandchildren not wanting to leave their grandparents. Really—are you kidding me?

I was about crazy—as there was nothing more that I could do! I told my granddaughter that she would have to tell her teacher if something would happen because I didn't know what more I could do to help her. Our granddaughter was kept from us again, probably for a couple months, as suspicion of physical abuse of our granddaughter and grandson was being investigated. Sad to say, but my daughter, as well as other parents, oftentimes use their children as little pawns, not letting grandparents see their grandchildren if they were upset over one thing or another. But of course they still want to keep connected in case they need us for something. After these two months went by and my granddaughter was able to see us again, she said, "I thought I would never get to see you and Papa again." What she was put through broke my heart. I was so desperate that I even wrote to Dr. Phil a couple times during this year but never heard back.

We found out later our granddaughter was often being confined to her room and would have to write letters downstairs to see if her and her brother, Brady, could come down. My daughter was insistent that the kids call each new boyfriend "Daddy." My granddaughter said to me during this time that her mom told her she has three dads: her real dad, James, Lyle, and also Kevin—but to not tell anyone else she is calling Kevin dad. My granddaughter said to me, "Grandma, I want to be a mommy someday—a good mommy."

Shortly after Christmas Eve of 2004, when we had all four of the children up to our house to spend some time with us, things began to fall apart very quickly. We had invited our daughter to come up with her children, but her then boyfriend, Lyle, (who later admitted in a report to having been involved in meth and also the abuser of our grandson) was not welcome at our house. So our daughter chose not to come if he was not welcome—but surprisingly did let us have all the children that day. They came to us very dirty, but we bathed them all and put on one of their Christmas presents so they had clean clothes to wear. We had a fun day with all of them! We found out later that these four children would spend all of the next day—Christmas Day—in their beds/bedrooms alone, with a lot of adults sleeping all over the place and that our grandson, Brady, was crying for his mom.

We knew that my daughter would probably be mad as we were taking some steps to set more strict boundaries at our home and that we were not going to be welcoming any more of her boyfriends into our home. We thought that she might hold the kids from us as we moved forward, and we were also concerned that the kids would be home from school during Christmas break. The day after Christmas, we discovered that our granddaughter, Kynnedi, had left her doll at our home—so her grandpa went to drop it by and told her he would drive by everyday around 10:00 in the morning and for her to wave from her bedroom window so that we knew she and her brothers were okay.

The next day, things really happened! My six-year-old granddaughter, Kynnedi, took it upon herself that morning to let people know by opening her upstairs window and yelling *"Help"*—which brought the police to the house very quickly. In the report, she was observed by neighbors hanging out a second-story window and crying and asking for help. Around 10:45 that morning, she said that her mom and boyfriend were asleep and would not get out of bed. According to the police report, there were five adults sleeping—my granddaughter said there had been eight or nine guys. A professional sent a message to the department that there were concerns regarding drug usage by my daughter and her newest boyfriend, Kevin.

My husband and I again did try to get our daughter some serious help and petitioned the court. She was court-ordered to attend inpatient day treatment throughout the week, and she did start to go but then didn't continue on a regular basis, therefore not benefitting her, and nothing was ever done to hold her accountable to that court order. After everyone had offered her much help and services, my daughter refused to listen to anyone and chose to leave the state for a period of time with her newest abusive boyfriend, Kevin. Eventually my daughter lost her children, and we were able to adopt our granddaughter, Kynnedi. I feel our family gave my daughter every opportunity to receive all the help from us and also from many community services, but she made the poor choices of her friends and the addictive lifestyle over her children. This was so very, very sad.

Watching what my grandchildren had to go through, for over three-plus years, was almost unbearable. Without God as my Rock, I would never have made it through. Finally my grandchildren were all safe, and I didn't have to worry about their care and safety anymore. My husband and I had the two babies, Michael and Zachery, for a couple months, along with our six-year-old granddaughter, Kynnedi, until a wonderful foster/adoptive home was found for the babies, ages one and two. We felt that we were just too old to take on three little children at our age, as my husband was getting ready to retire. We were even told that we might lose our granddaughter if we didn't take all three of them. You see, we really did fall in love with these two little guys while they were in our care, but we felt they needed younger parents able to be more involved with them as they grew up.

So we made the hard decision to move forward with this wonderful younger family adopting our two little grandsons. Before they left our care we had them baptized and also had a family farewell birthday party for them. Then a year or so later, these little guys ended up moving across the country, so we weren't able to see them very often. But we did make several trips out West to see them, along with Kynnedi and also other family members who went along. Our grandsons would sometimes come back here to visit us, too. We have, over the years, had a wonderful relationship with the boy's adoptive parents and their little boy, who is another grandson to us. We have taken family vacations together and spent Christmases together. I am so very thankful to God for the wonderful lives these boys have had, and I've shared that with them as they have become older and they have had questions.

It was very hard to see my daughter lose her children, but she had been given so much help and opportunity to turn her life around, but she didn't seem to really care at that point. I wish there wouldn't have been so many people continuing to enable our daughter. Maybe she would have had to really look at herself and her situation and gotten the help she needed. As I look back, I did do some enabling as I tried to help my grandkids, but I saw no other way as they could not take care of themselves. I always had the front row seat to the pain and frightening life I saw my grandchildren going through, with little being done to change things and no one doing anything to help them. They were just little babies six years of age and under—and there were four of them, which would be a handful for any mom, even at her best. My daughter, Heidi, was stubborn and not willing to listen to us or anyone else to really understand or see the dangers to her children. This book is truly written from the heart of a mom and grandmother who loved them all so very much!

I was so happy for my grandchildren to have a chance at a much better, safer life! I had always said that I would have given them all up to never see them again—if that was what it would have taken for them to be well taken care of and safe! I was sad for my daughter, as I had wanted and prayed for a different outcome for her and her children, but she made the choices she did, and she would now have to live with those choices.

I had not planned to share all the realness of those days because it is still very painful as I look back at my notes of the things my grandchildren said to me when they were little, and also through others' notes and reports. I hope by reliving this, I will make come to life what these little children lived in and went through, giving them also a voice in those early years. I also hope to help people understand that we must do more and earlier as family members and agencies for children at risk. I had started early on to document and date a lot of what I was seeing, as I knew the situation was not good, and these children might need to have a voice and facts if ever needed. Unfortunately, grandparents have no rights in our state and often are listened to the least.

Also, I hope it gives some insight into homes that children live in today where they can't speak up for themselves. I feel we must do a better job of addressing situations sooner—rather than later—as these very early formative years are so important for children! Even though my relationship with my daughter was never very good during these years—and I kind of had to divorce and separate from my daughter—I would never change what I had to do for my grandchildren! I would do it all over again to take a stand for these little ones to try to save them and give them a better life.

Chapter 6

Raising Our Granddaughter

*T*o be able to help our dear special granddaughter, Kynnedi—and the wonderful beautiful young girl she was and is—was a blessing! We are so glad we were able to be there for her, but wish it could have turned out so differently for her. We always wanted our daughter, Heidi, to be able to raise her own daughter, and we would have been happy just being Kynnedi's grandparents. I had prayed that our daughter would get the help she needed so she would be able to raise her own children and we could just walk alongside them.

Our granddaughter had to have been so very confused as she saw entirely different ways of living between her mom's house and our home. She had learned in Sunday school that you were to listen and respect your parents but was being told to lie and saw stealing and things that were wrong going on when she was with her mom. A little later, we were seeing some anger issues and found out that our daughter had taken our granddaughter to the hospital for some behavior concerns a few years back. The doctor told Heidi to stabilize her life for this little girl's sake, and my daughter had failed to do that. Early on, my granddaughter had been given a diagnosis of borderline oppositional defiance disorder—as she had been defying the situations at her mother's house, but that was because she knew that these things were wrong. She had told me once that she had been with her mom when she went into the bathroom at a store, and saw her mom put some things from the store in the diaper bag. How sad that my granddaughter had to be the one to know right from wrong and, as a little girl, take a stand. With many years of counseling, to undo the hurt that was done to this little girl, we did not see any serious issues. Her papa and I are glad that we were able to be a positive influence in her life!

We had our granddaughter, Kynnedi, and her two little baby brothers, Michael and Zachery, for about two months. When it became obvious that my daughter was not working to get her children back, we knew we could not parent three little children over the long term at our age. We felt we were just too old to undertake this long-term commitment. We did fall in love with these two little baby boys once they were in our home, but we felt these babies needed much younger parents who could really engage with them and be able to do more things with them. So these boys were placed in foster-to-adopt care and were adopted by a wonderful young couple who had a little boy.

Our relationship with these parents was like having a couple more of our own children. We so much appreciate their devotion and love for our two grandsons! We could not have found another couple who could have loved them any more—and like I said earlier, their birth son is another one of our grandsons. We are blessed beyond measure to see that we have been able to blend our families so well together! I believe my husband and I probably could have survived and managed with all three children, but I don't think we could have given all three children the time and attention and everything they really needed. We were told later, by a specialist, that it was wise that our granddaughter was adopted alone as she needed that extra special one on one attention. So we hope our two grandsons, Michael and Zachery, realize and truly understand that we loved them enough to look at what was best for them and don't ever think that we didn't love or care about them.

With our granddaughter, Kynnedi, we were hoping to divide parenting and grand-parenting up, but once you become a parent again, even though it's your grandchild, it doesn't quite work that way. Part of me just wanted to be a grandma to my first grandchild—although I feel blessed to have been able to be there for her as her parent too—to guide and direct her! I do feel my husband and I did miss the joy of just being her grandparents, and she has missed the joy of having us just be her grandparents, which I feel she also needed. We didn't just get to spoil her and send her home. Most of you probably won't understand what I am saying, unless you have walked in our shoes! Our job was to be her parents first and foremost, and that took some of the *fun* out of being grandparents!

The first year and a half was a little rocky, as our granddaughter had to adjust to her mom abandoning her, and living without all three of her little brothers being with her. She had to learn that we were her caretakers and that she was not the parent in charge of everything. Then she was faced with the sudden death of her little brother, Brady, whom she had mothered. On top of that, she had to deal with her two baby brothers moving so far away from her. Our granddaughter would be so scared when we would go out someplace that Lyle, her mom's scariest boyfriend, would show up or that we might be driving close to his place if we were out of town.

Our granddaughter was very hurt and angry—which she had every right to be—and it took some time for her to overcome it. With much therapy, a loving cat of her own, art drawings, a punching bag, journaling—and my husband and I trying to learn new ways of trying to address things—we were able to move past this behavior. I feel I could do things so much better today if I had known all the information I have learned about adverse childhood experiences (ACEs) and trauma in children. This would have also been very helpful in my dealing with Heidi's issues to better understand what she was going through with the trauma of her being sexually abused.

During the first year and a half, Heidi was coming to see our granddaughter occasionally at our home, and we were very open to this. The second Christmas came, and my daughter wanted to see her daughter at the last minute, but we already had made plans. I suggested she come up a couple of days later to bring gifts to Kynnedi, instead of just dropping them off, and to also spend some time with her. This made my daughter mad, so she didn't call during my granddaughter's school break to set anything up for a visit. This disappointed my granddaughter, so I decided things were going to have to change to make sure this didn't happen again and that my granddaughter wasn't hurt by her mom's inconsistency. My granddaughter said to me, "I'll just buy a gift at your store, Grandma. That way if my mom doesn't show up, I can just take it back." My heart hurt for this little girl. I was thinking we needed to bring my granddaughter's therapist into this, to set some guidelines.

A couple of times in the next couple of years or so, Heidi did call to see if she could see her daughter, and I told her yes if she was willing to work things out with Kynnedi's therapist so that she could set some boundaries and be willing to tell her daughter the truth if she were to ask questions. My daughter did go once but didn't like the therapist and what she had to say and refused to go back. I tried to talk to my daughter that this wasn't about her—that it was about her little girl—but she just didn't understand. My granddaughter had wanted to ask her mom two questions; "Why did you leave us kids for your friends?" and "What happened to my brother?" I'm not sure as she got older that these questions were as important to her, but at that time they were. So my daughter's refusal to work with my granddaughter and her therapist in order for regular, face-to-face contact to happen came to a standstill. For a while my daughter would make occasional phone calls or send cards or letters, but when my granddaughter turned thirteen, this all stopped—even birthday cards.

By now our granddaughter had a new little half-sister that I felt bad that she didn't know, and I thought this little girl could really benefit from knowing her big sister. We did try to address this with Kynnedi's therapist every six months or so. We did not have great expectations that our daughter would work with this therapist anymore, but we were trying to work out a way for our granddaughter, her mom, and her half-sister, to have some kind of a relationship—while making sure the girls wouldn't be hurt in the middle of it. The therapist did not think that a reunion would have been the best for our grand-daughter but was willing to bring it up. Our granddaughter at that time was a teenager involved in her busy school life, and she wasn't sure how this was going to look or happen, so it never did. Thankfully, my granddaughter has been able to move on past all of this and forgive her mom.

Our granddaughter was a very mature, very self-directed child, doing well in school. She was involved in many things throughout her school years, had many friends, and was very well liked. I believe my husband and I gave her a good life, but she feels I was obsessively strict. Could I have been, after learning of the things that happened to her mom? Also, after what my older kids told me they had pulled sometimes? Probably! I do know and admit that I was very protective of her, but I wanted to make sure nothing would ever happen to hurt my granddaughter any more than she had already been hurt.

My husband and I felt our granddaughter was sometimes embarrassed by us, since we were older, but then remember that our own kids were probably embarrassed by us at the middle school age too. We were so very proud of Kynnedi, for her hard work and determination in being the best person she could be! She made our job much easier! Her parents had messed up, but she was determined that she was going to show everyone that she was going to be someone much different, almost expecting perfection of herself! She certainly has accomplished amazing things and was an excellent student throughout school, always on the honor roll and involved in many activities in and out of school which she enjoyed, such as Awana, dance, band, and choir. She was also involved in many sports, such as soccer, softball, track, and golf, which she did well in. As she went on to college, she was on the Dean's list, with straight A's, and graduated college early with a criminology degree!

We have gone through some bumps in the road, especially when her mom passed away suddenly. I will go into a little more details about my daughter's death a little later in this book. Our granddaughter, Kynnedi, was angry that we hadn't done more to help her mom, but as time went on, she seemed to realize that we had done many things, and the reason she had not had contact with her mom through her years growing up was that her mom was not willing to work with our granddaughter's therapist to keep her from getting emotionally hurt any further. At the time I really believed I had done the right thing for my granddaughter's protection, but I did second guess that after my daughter's sudden death.

I am so very proud of my granddaughter, having overcome all the obstacles that she has had to deal with to make such a wonderful, productive life for herself. We have helped by loving her and guiding her, but she has been the strongest to have gone through all these overwhelming things and to have come out on top! She is definitely a survivor and so amazing! Many people have given my husband and me the credit, but I believe our granddaughter deserves the credit. When she was nine and ten years old, Kynnedi had written two different songs for two child abuse awareness concerts. She has always had a gift to write down her thoughts on paper, which has probably helped her to make it through the tough times in her life. A sweet man, named Dave, put her two songs to music, and they performed together. One was called "A Good Move," and the other one was "My Hero." I have included them:

A GOOD MOVE

I'm 9 years old: I used to care for my brothers, cuz my mama sometimes would forget—I'd change their diapers and feed all 3 their bottles...That was back when I was 6.

One day mama's friend—hit my brother who was 4—and I told Mom I DIDN'T want to live there anymore.

I made a GOOD MOVE to my GRANDPARENT'S house—was the BEST DAY OF MY LIFE. They treat me like a tree—feed and care for me. And I feel GREAT—I FEEL safe—I HUG them every day—for helping me make, such a GOOD MOVE.

I don't have to live with cigarettes and strangers—I don't have to worry anymore. I don't have to be a mommy to my brothers—that's not what sisters are for.

Sometimes I still cry—but NOW it's happy tears—CUZ I'm living where I never HAVE to hide my FEARS.

I made a GOOD MOVE to my GRANDPARENT'S house—was the BEST DAY OF MY LIFE. They treat me like a tree—feed and care for me. And I feel GREAT—I FEEL safe—I HUG them every day—for helping me make, such a GOOD MOVE.

Gramma and Grandpa—You came to my rescue—You are my heroes. Do you know how much I LOVE YOU?

It was a GOOD MOVE... Coming to your house...Was the BEST DAY of my life. You treat me like a tree—feed and care for me. And I feel GREAT; I FEEL safe. THANK YOU for helping me make—such a GOOD MOVE—yea!

MY HERO

My he-ro
Flying in to rescue me,
Helping me to BREATHE on my own,
Throwing me a rope, Saving me with hope

My he-ro
You heard me—when I was calling
Caught me—when I was falling

My he-ro
You've been a good friend to me,
Teaching me to stand on my own,
Taking off the rope, Holding me with hope

My he-ro
You mean so many things to me—Mo-ther, tea-cher,
fa-ther, prea-cher
Shining like a light, My own northern star,
But your act of courage Makes you who you are

My he-ro
An angel who appeared to me, Watching till I FLY on my own,
Giving me the rope SO I CAN bring others hope.

My He-ro

My granddaughter has accomplished so many things for such a
young person. She plays the piano beautifully! We bought the
piano for her after her little brother died, and it has been good
therapy for her! She started writing a book in grade school and

published it in middle school. Her grade school counselor was very helpful in encouraging her to write. My granddaughter and I were fortunate to be invited to go with a dear friend and her husband and family to Cancun, Mexico when she was in middle school, and I will always treasure the memories of this special time together.

My granddaughter is a leader and a wonderful example for overcoming much adversity in her life. She has moved beyond her disappointments and hurts to have a beautiful life and has done well in whatever she chooses to do, always giving her best—and also her viewpoint! Her grandpa and I are so very proud of her and her many accomplishments. She is very smart, strong-willed, and passionate for what she believes in and has a kind, loving, compassionate heart! Her beauty on the outside is matched by her wonderful Christ-like inner beauty. God has certainly had his hand on this beautiful child from the day she was born and has been watching over her. She is so very *special* to us and definitely is a "He-ro" to me and her grandpa! I am so very grateful for God's protection and guidance of my granddaughter's life from very little on!

A letter I wrote to my granddaughter on her graduation from high school:

> Kynnedi, Our Granddaughter & Daughter
> All in One,
>
> My hopes and prayers were always about what was best for you and although your life has not been quite the traditional one for you, I believe you had the best life that you could have under the circumstances. You took everything that came about and dealt with it, overcoming all

the adversities in your young life and striving to be the best that you could be through it all. You worked very hard, with much determination, to overcome the obstacles to prove that you could do it, and you did a wonderful job!

God had His hand on you and watched over you and your brothers from the day you were born. Grandma is so grateful, and I thank him always for the blessing that you have been in Grandpa's and my lives!

I've had to become your mom for the last twelve years, and sometimes—actually many times— we haven't agreed, and you have argued about my old-fashioned ways. I believe though that you always knew I loved you and wanted what was best for you. I know I was overprotective, but that's just being Grandma—right?

I am glad I was able to be there for you as your mom, but I have missed being your grandma and I think you have missed that too. I hope as we move forward into your college years and adult life that I can be more of the grandma that you need.

I love you with all my heart and soul, and we are so very proud of the special, beautiful, talented, wonderful, Christian young woman that you have become! We guided you, nurtured, and loved you all along the way, but you did the hardest work to overcome everything that was dealt to you and have made a wonderful success story that you deserve the credit for.

The years have gone by so very fast as we watched you grow and tried to keep up with everything you were involved in. Although at times we would be physically worn out, we were very happy that we could be there for you when you really needed us.

As you grow up and graduate, your future is in your hands—hopefully directed by God guiding you. I can't wait to see what lies in store for you as you partner with the loving Lord throughout your life!

Love You Always & Forever,
Grandma and Grandpa too

Chapter 7

Losing Our Little Grandson

*T*he loss of our first grandson, Brady, Kynnedi's little brother, ten days before turning five, of an accident due to dehydration of diabetes insipidus, was very hard for me to deal with. The call came in the early hours of an August morning. This little boy's life was not very fair to start with, yet I knew Jesus took him home to be safe and to take care of him.

I didn't foresee a real change in his life too much after going to live with his dad—maybe at first it was better, but for the long haul I didn't think it would be good. I believe he would have always struggled and fallen through the cracks. I felt Jesus was telling me that no one would ever take care of him very well—and that He was taking this little boy home with Him to give him the care he needed and deserved. This little boy has suffered so much in the care of both of his parents. He deserved so much more than he ever received. Even when his mom and dad were together and things were at its best, it was minimal parenting!

Brady had spent time with us, and we saw many concerning things that we tried to address. It broke my heart to see the neglect and how he was mistreated. It is so very sad, as I share this, that he had to die to be safe and at peace. There had been many years of worry and tears over this little boy. I finally didn't have to worry anymore.

Our little grandson was developmentally delayed, some from his early birth and some from the situations he lived in. He also had a mild case of cerebral palsy. He struggled to try to tell me things in his limited vocabulary, trying to say he was being hurt and not wanting to go home to either parent's house. When at his mom's house, he would hold on to me and not want me to leave, also telling me one time when having a play day at my house that the boyfriend, Lyle, hit him and hurt him, as he lifted up his pant legs and pointed to his knee with a bruise and pointed to his back and his butt. There was also a time that Brady was spending some extended time at his dad's place before going there to live permanently, when my daughter Heidi brought him into my store and said that he came back from his dad's this way. Brady was limping and had three bruises on his left side and a small bruise on his left right cheek, as well as some bruises on his back. Over the years I found all of the parents lied and played games with the kids, so I never knew who was telling the truth.

Often when taking Brady back to his dad's, after moving there, he would start crying and saying, "Me don't want to go home to daddy's and his girlfriend's." The minute I would pull up at their house, he would stop crying as though he knew he had to or he wouldn't be able to go with me again. Another time, he had been taken to the emergency room for an infection of his penis, and there was suspicion as to what had happened. My daughter was supposed to have a prescription filled for this little guy but didn't fill his prescription until four days later.

At his last Christmas program at preschool, he was like a wild animal, completely out of control. As I had mentioned earlier, there were witnesses on occasion of the one boyfriend telling him to get his f...ing butt off the school bus. I did not know this until after his death. As much as the school, the Department of Human Services, and his doctors knew of our concerns as grandparents, nobody did anything. We were told it had to get worse before anything could be done and that we had the best of the worst! I had always feared all four of these children would be dead before anyone would really intervene to help my grandchildren—and now one grandchild was dead!

The environment, especially the last few months living with my daughter, Heidi, was extremely concerning for Brady and his little brothers, Michael and Zachery, and his older sister, Kynnedi. Our grandson, Brady, spent much of his time double-gated in his room alone with bars on his window, supposedly to keep him safe. He had nothing on his walls and nothing in his room to play with, and he had no sheets, pillow, or blankets to sleep with. Sometimes he was naked in his room, according to a report I read later. He would also mess himself and smear it all over his walls. I guess when no one pays attention to you, and you have nothing to do all day and are kept in your room most of the time and not allowed out to go to the bathroom, what would we expect of this little boy? One time, the paternal grandparents stopped by and were horrified by the condition of his room, and they did report it. The newest boyfriend, Lyle, was abusing him and then there were concerns of how he was being fed. He developed a rare illness: diabetes insipidus, water diabetes. We are not sure of how or why he got it, and there were many concerns as to how he was treated and the concerns surrounding his early death.

There were many concerns, over the months, after my grandson went to live at his dad's house. Of course, I didn't know until later that there were two investigations in another state they lived in with concerns of inconsistencies in the stories told. One was a suspicious broken arm, reportedly falling down the steps. Both reports came back, labeled unfounded. Brady had also been gravely ill in the spring, six months before he died, and had been admitted to a large hospital with extremely high sodium levels. They thought he would not survive. This hospital said they had never seen a child survive with levels that high. He did recover after several weeks in the hospital but had to relearn to walk and talk all over again. What really happened there? We don't really know. Why wouldn't Brady's dad take extra special care of him after he went through all this?

I had witnessed something very concerning one Sunday morning when I went to pick Brady up to take him to Sunday school and church and he wasn't ready. His stepmom was sitting Indian style on the table (she was a bigger woman), and she was making Brady eat a dry pop tart, without allowing him to have anything to drink while he is crying and choking. She was pinching his cheeks to make him swallow his food. I did report this to his doctor as I knew he was to have a follow-up checkup for his diabetes insipidus, and I was very concerned with what I saw. I saw this to be bizarre and extreme! The stepmom and his dad told all of us grandparents that our grandson was to have a strict, "doctor ordered" limited water intake, but we found out later we were told lies, and it was the parent's orders because Brady had gulped a whole lot of water down and got sick. This had made the stepmom mad, so this was her rule.

I also found in reports later that my grandson's speech and occupational therapist had reached out to the parents and had sent a letter to the doctor that they were very concerned with the four-ounce limit of water in a three to four hour period, saying that was not enough for this child and they were seeing signs of dehydration. They were seeing him being obsessed with water as he watched other children drink, and one time he had vomited a large mass of food at a therapy session. The therapist believed he may have stopped breathing. Still, the parents would not allow additional water, and the doctor had sent back a letter, saying the therapist should go by the stepmom's water restriction. The therapists were also questioning the parents about the many bruises as well.

It was shared with us after his death that at his dad's house a neighbor witnessed him standing in the corner and being locked in his room for hours as punishment—sometimes all day, with a lock on the outside of the door. She also reported that he would be drinking out of the toilet. One night when this neighbor's teenage daughter would go camping with my grandson and this family, she would witness my grandson being yelled at and threatened to be thrown in the river if he didn't shut up. Also, this neighbor shared that the stepmom would blast out screams at Brady and that she said that she would have his dad blister his ass because he would not do what he was told.

In a report later, on the morning of my grandson's death, a neighbor had said she had stopped by my grandson's house and told the stepmom that Brady did not look very good, as he had a bluish color, and that they should call the doctor and take him in to have his sodium level checked. The parents said he always appeared that way, and it was just the way the sleeper he had on made him look. The parents said he was having some behaviors and messing his pants. This neighbor, who had some nursing experience, said that wasn't normal and that something was wrong, but instead of calling the doctor and taking him in that day to be checked, they instead called to set up an appointment for him to be seen later for his behaviors. The stepmom had told the neighbor later that my grandson was so defiant on that day that she had his dad clean up the mess. There were all these signs of his sodium level being high, so why didn't they take him to the doctor?

Later that day, we found out that the paternal grandparents had called to talk to Brady and said that he didn't sound very good. His voice sounded funny, rather weak, and when they would try to talk to him, all he would say was, "I pooped my pants." They said he sounded very stressed and frail. These grandparents voiced their concerns to their son, Chance, Brady's dad. He said they were eating supper, and he would call them back. These grandparents have blamed themselves for not just stopping by that night to see how he was doing, instead of waiting for that phone call.

That return phone call didn't come until the middle of the night at 2:00 a.m., and Brady was dead. The autopsy was not completed until five months later and said he died in his sleep at 11:30 that night, dying of an accident due to dehydration of diabetes insipidus with cerebral palsy and acute mixed drugs (trazodone, amphetamine, and dextromethorphan) intoxication with multiple bruises on his upper torso. The stepmom said that she had seen him still alive at 11:00 p.m. She also said that he had been awake for seventy-two hours and had had trouble breathing earlier in the evening. No resuscitation efforts were attempted. I have concerns of how you can die of an accident due to dehydration when you live a few blocks away from a hospital and a clinic. Also, all the signs were there that he needed care, as he was struggling to breathe earlier that evening and should have been taken to the doctor or hospital. However, nobody bothered to take him. To think that my grandson was struggling to breathe and had to die alone in his bedroom is very hard to take.

I had called the day before to check on Brady, as he had been in the hospital the previous weekend and he was supposed to have gone back for a checkup the middle of the week. We found out later the parents had not taken him for this checkup. Why? I was told he was having some behaviors, and I asked if I could take him for a while, but they declined my offer. His diabetes insipidus was not a life-threatening illness but did need to be seriously monitored, and the parents knew what to look for and what to do if they saw the signs and they were: acting out behaviors and not sleeping. We also found out later, through reports, that the parents didn't like to have to be at the hospital, especially on the weekends, and to have to sit with him while they administered fluids and monitored his sodium levels. Also, the emergency room doctors were questioning them about all of his many bruises. So if Brady had problems, they would often wait until Monday so they wouldn't be questioned by the emergency room doctor and nurses, and he would just be able to see his regular doctor. Also on the day of his death, the stepmom had plans to go somewhere for the afternoon and evening.

The day of Brady's death and several days after, we were having people tell us these unbelievable things. Of course, after he was gone, people came forward to tell us these things. Why couldn't they have told us these things and told the appropriate people who could have helped him? Would anybody have done anything to have made a difference for him and helped him if people had come forward sooner? Who knows? I know how very frustrated I was and had been—and the many things that I had been seeing myself for weeks, months, and years at both parent's houses. Many people knew the situations, as we were told later, but yet they did *nothing*! Our grandson's school told a person known to us not to mention anything to us about concerns. The bus driver sharing that when they would go to drop Brady off at his mom's house after preschool, he would be so excited to see his house but then would become upset when his mom and her boyfriend came out to get him off the bus. This boyfriend, I found out later, had a founded abuse charge for hurting my grandson.

In talking with Brady's dad, the evening we made the funeral arrangements, he said that he was sorry that he didn't take better care of Brady. He said to me that all he remembers the night Brady died was that he had spanked his butt three times that day for messing his pants. According to his dad, he put Brady to bed at 8:00 that evening, and he threw a tantrum. The stepmom said when she came home around 10:00 p.m. that Brady got up to go to the bathroom and he was kicking. She said she gave him his medication at 10:30 p.m. and put him back to bed. He was screaming at first and went back into his room around 11:00 p.m., and he had fallen asleep. I believe on this day, when all these things were happening, this little boy's body was shutting down, and these parents didn't even bother to get him to a doctor. In hearing things that were told to me and the funeral home being concerned about the many bruises on his body, an investigation was opened with many people being interviewed, but when completed, it came back unfounded.

What this little boy had to go through was horrible! I went through a very hard first year after his death because no one was being held accountable for the neglect that led to his death that night. The parents said they wouldn't have done anything differently that day. What? A child is dead—and you wouldn't have changed anything you did that day or night? I went through extreme sadness and some depression and a lot of anger at people for not doing more to help him when he was alive—and then not holding anyone accountable after he had died. He was just considered a nobody's child in the eyes of so many, yet he was such a precious little boy who had not been given much of a chance at life by either of his own parents. I truly believe that for many months, my grandson had lived and struggled with many signs of—and on the verge—of dehydration. He had shown many signs of desperation by his obsession with water, even to the extreme of drinking out of the toilet. How very sad that he had to live and struggle like that and that we couldn't have done more to help him. Brady had struggled, fighting and surviving to overcome so much and then he wasn't even able to make it to five years of age.

The week leading up to my grandson's death, my granddaughter and I had been reading this book about heaven, called *What About Heaven*, written by Kathleen Long Bostrom. The morning of her brother's death, I was so afraid to have to tell my little seven-year-old granddaughter what had happened, as she already had to deal with so very much. She had been a little mommy and protector to him, and he was like her son. She loved him so very much. They had been so close. How was she going to take this? I started out that morning by talking about this book that we had been reading about heaven and asked her what she thought heaven would be like. As I look back, I think God had been preparing her and me for what was going to happen, as she had wanted to read this book twice that week. After telling her the sad news, I held her, and we cried and talked some. I suggested she might want to write down her thoughts and also draw a picture to help with her sadness.

My granddaughter wrote this note and read it the following Sunday at our church.

> Dear Brady, I hope you have a better life in heaven. When you get in heaven, you aren't sike (sic) no more. You don't get hurt no more. I hope you reneder (sic) all of us. I love you Brady.

After reaching out for a year and trying to address these concerns at the highest of levels in my city and state, I had to let go of it, or it would have destroyed me! The official who had called me a crazy grandma way back, even reached out to let me know of a grief camp for my granddaughter. I wonder if he was feeling a little guilty now. I finally was able to let it go and get justice for my grandson, Brady, by educating and bringing awareness in my church and community to the needs of children and what they might be going through—and taking a stand for other kids to try to help them. It took me many years to move on and forgive the people who were the caretakers of this little boy, including my own daughter. Thank God, her son, Brady, didn't die in her care. If only she would have dealt with her own issues, she wouldn't have lost her son to begin with. I realized I had to let go of it all for my own sake.

In memory of this little boy we do special things in our community for children, such as giving out ice cream in his memory; school supplies; clothing, mittens, and hats for children starting school; and also books and red balloons. We also placed a beautiful red (Brady's favorite color) bench down at the playground where so many local children go to play. This playground was my grandson, Brady's, favorite place to go and the very last place we had been to spend a special fun day with him! I remember him having so much fun on the merry-go-round, although that day, I noticed multiple bruises in various stages on his chest and stomach when he had lifted up his shirt, and he also had a black eye. I did take a picture and drop it by the next day to our local department, DHS, and found out later that it had already been reported and was under investigation—which later was considered unfounded.

Were there early signs that should have been caught and something done? Had my grandson been trying to tell us something all along in his limited speech? My grandson's life was so very, very sad. I saw this little boy being forced to eat a dry pop tart without anything to drink—choking and crying and asking for a drink.

Others had noticed this locally and reached out to try to address this, even writing a letter to his doctor saying that the limited water by the parents was not enough to sustain him properly and that they were seeing signs of dehydration, but nothing changed. Of course, we did not find out many of these things until after his death.

Why didn't anyone help this little boy sooner—and speak up? Both sets of us grandparents have always questioned why these adults were never held accountable for neglecting to get him the care that he needed that day. We also feel incredibly bad to think that we believed these parents and went along with some of the things that we were told. It is so sad to think a child has to die to be safe, taken care of, and not afraid, isn't it?

The Letter I Read at My Grandson's Funeral

My Dearest First Grandson, Brady,

You are such a special, sweet little boy. Your very short life here on earth wasn't what it should have been. You were given so many physical challenges to deal with from the day you were born, sweetheart. I hope that you know (and I believe that you did) that you were loved by many people—especially your grandparents and big sissy, Kynnedi. I tried to be there for you as often as I could and wish it could have been more. I'm so glad for the special times and memories I have of being with you, especially this past week that sissy and I spent with you at the hospital. We walked the halls, talked, and played with you, and we lifted you up to the window to watch the cars and trucks. We read your favorite book, *Clifford the Big Red Dog*. Grandma rocked you and sang, "Jesus Loves You," Brady, because the Bible tells Grandma so and "Jesus loves the Little Children" all the little Brady's of the world. We gave you the special stuffed dog we brought you that you loved and slept with. Jesus loves you so much, precious little boy, that He didn't want for you to suffer any longer. He saw you suffering in so many ways, and nobody was able to take care of all your needs—and He knew He could. So now, little angel, you are able to walk and talk and run and be happy! You are safe and free from any hurt or pain. You'll never be angry ever again or be poked with a needle or take medication or wear braces You were so very brave and strong. You are now free from all of this and can really be the little boy you weren't able to be here.

We will always remember you for the love, the hugs and kisses you gave, for your sweet little smile and your dimples. We saw the other side of you also—the orneriness and stubbornness that tried our patience—but you had much reason for your anger, for you struggled to come back from several illnesses and problems, and you certainly weren't given a normal little boy's life. Grandma's heart breaks for what you had to go through, and your little life should have been so much better. Now it can and will be.

We will always remember you being the happiest blowing bubbles and playing with the bubble lawn mower and playing in the basement at Grandma and Papa's house with your cousins and sissy, reading books like *Clifford the Big Red Dog* and *The Big Brown Bear*. I remember the slumber party we had last winter with you, sissy, and your cousins when everyone else was sleeping. You said, "Mamo, I awake, I awake." You loved to watch the *Wiggles* and *Nemo*. You really tried to learn your colors, and to help you, we would play a game at the stoplights with green to go and red to stop. Red was your favorite color. You loved to go to Sunday school and go up the big hill to church. You always wanted a drink of water and would always figure out a way to get to it or take it. You loved your little brothers, Michael and Zachery, and although you didn't see them very often, you always remembered them and hugged and kissed them. You especially loved your big sissy, Kynnedi. Your eyes would light up whenever she was around. She was mommy to you and loved you so much and tried to protect you. You also loved your stepbrother and stepsisters.

We will always think about you and will miss you so very much, but know you are now in the loving arms of Jesus—free from pain and fear. Someday we are promised to see you again in heaven, but we do have to do something for that to happen. We need to acknowledge that Jesus lived and died for each of us; we have to admit we've done wrong and sinned and ask for His forgiveness and then turn our lives over to Him. We are promised eternal life together with you precious, Brady, and when that day comes and we can see you smiling and happy, free from all pain—blowing your bubbles in heaven—we'll then understand why you were taken at such an early age.

God thank you for being my Rock and Strength through all of this! I thank you heavenly Father for watching over this little boy. I had to trust You that You were always there watching over this little boy and comforting him in his pain. Goodbye for now, precious little Brady, Grandma loves you and will see and hold you again. I trust in God's promises to me that I will see you again, for He always keeps His promises. You'll be my little angel in heaven.

Love, Grandma

Chapter 8

Our Youngest Daughter's Sudden Death

The sudden death of our youngest daughter, Heidi—dying in her sleep at age forty was such a shock to my husband and me. Her autopsy revealed that she had died of cardiac arrhythmia due to severe coronary artery disease, with tobacco contributing to her death. She had lived so much of her life not taking proper care of her health, and I also believe her early alcohol and drug use played a part of her deteriorating health. We certainly never thought we would lose her at such a young age. It was very noticeable that the many years of self-destructive behavior had played a heavy toll on her life—and that was very hard to see as her mom. I loved my youngest daughter with all my heart, but she broke my heart so many times by the poor choices she made for her life and for the lives of her children. Needless to say, our relationship was a very rocky one for many years!

From a very young age, I had concerns about my youngest daughter as she struggled to express herself verbally, as a little girl, and her struggles in school. Even with the extra help we were able to get for her and the positive support of family, she still seemed to struggle socially and academically. We had a speech therapist to help her, private school, and tutoring. I was a very strong advocate for her in the public school—as often they were gloom and doom—telling me when she was a kindergartner that she would never learn to read or write, which I thought was so unfair and cruel, as she was just a little girl starting to learn. Her kindergarten teacher was not a good match for her at all; she was kind of a cold drill sergeant and not the loving, positive kind of teacher that would have been a comfort to my daughter. My daughter was very close to me as a little girl and had a hard time leaving me, especially to go off to someone who was not very warm and affectionate her first year of school. Her professional therapist later told us that this beginning school experience for our daughter could have deeply affected her for her entire life.

We had started our youngest daughter in public kindergarten, but because of the teacher and her regressing (starting to stutter in school after first starting, not being able to share things at school that she was sharing with us at home), we moved her to a private Christian school in the middle of her kindergarten year, where she did pretty well. Her first grade year went well. Her teacher was an older, warm, and loving grandma-type lady. My daughter struggled in learning phonics, but she was able to learn words from memory, so she was able to do okay. We did move her back to public school to repeat second grade and for some of the extra help that the public school had to offer. As a young girl we also involved her in dance classes for more social time with other girls and she also played softball.

Then our oldest daughter, Danielle, went off to college. Like I said earlier, this is something I have always regretted doing. I wish I would have kept my youngest daughter at the private school. My daughter, Heidi, was able to get through grade school okay but struggled with comprehension. She did go on to be a pretty good reader and writer. In grade school, we worked with a couple of teachers to prepare our daughter for middle school and then placed her in a couple of classes to qualify her for some extra help in the resource room—which unfortunately put her in with behavioral kids. I continued to have to confront the school on things, trying to best advocate for her throughout middle school. When Heidi moved into high school things were a little better, and she was even on the swim team her freshman year and did pretty well.

Around eighth grade, we were looking at behavior problems, which continued throughout her school years and after! Heidi's desire to fit in throughout her teen years led her to be attracted to kids who had no boundaries or rules, and who also had very enabling parents. I believe she also was jealous of her older sister and brother, as she saw them as having a much easier life than she had—in school and in everything. Up to this point we were unaware of her being sexually abused. Thus was the beginning of the many years of heartache and heartbreak for our daughter and eventually her four children.

When I learned someone we knew sexually abused my daughter, I had a very hard time understanding how anyone could do such a thing to a child. We saw much acting out from my daughter as she entered the teen years and into her adult life, as this person was never held accountable for what he did to her. I feel this was a big part of my daughter's destructive lifestyle throughout her life. We had even considered moving out of our home and this neighborhood, but the therapist, in talking with our daughter, felt that she might feel safer staying here and knowing where he was.

We had given her many years of therapy to try to help her overcome the sexual abuse—trying to help her work through her problems—but nothing seemed to help her get past it. She chose and followed friends who were living a life of drugs and irresponsible behavior, and my daughter eventually chose that lifestyle for herself. Did she find it easier that way? Eventually my four grandchildren were caught up in the middle of all this craziness and dysfunction, with very scary adults surrounding them. What could my daughter possibly be thinking—or was she even thinking at all? I believe Heidi knew we would always love her no matter what she did.

It was so devastating to watch my grandchildren live like they did and my daughter not willing to listen to any of our family or to anyone's advice to make better choices! I tried to talk to my daughter many times about the safety of her children and to get the help she needed in order to put her children first. But my daughter was very stubborn and chose her friends over her children and their safety over and over again. Did my daughter knowingly do that, or were mental illness and/or drugs taking over? This is something we will never know.

A phone call in the early winter of 2005, brought 3 little children ages six, thirteen months, and twenty-two months to our home within an hour's notice. While we didn't have to worry about our grandchildren's safety anymore, we were physically exhausted at the end of each day—getting up very early in the morning and crashing in bed at night. My husband and I were still working full time, and I had to drive way across town in the middle of winter to have an available babysitter, which I had to seek out and find after having family and friends help out for a couple weeks until a sitter could be found. The two little babies' father was going to help out with babysitting, but he didn't even show up the first day. After many services were made available to my daughter to help her have her children returned, she refused and left the state with her newest boyfriend, abandoning her four children. Since her children were so very young, termination happened very quickly, and she lost custody of three of her children, and Brady went to live with his dad.

If I had known what was ahead of me, I would have said no way could I have gone through these things. My strong faith has helped me to realize that Jesus was carrying me and holding me in His loving arms through these tragic events. Through my pain, I have felt God's love, peace, and His presence. I trusted that God knew what was best even though I didn't understand—and it was far from what I prayed for or would have wanted to happen to my grandson, Brady, and my daughter, Heidi. Over time, I have learned to let go and let God, trusting in Him to be in charge of my life and to know what is best for me and my loved ones. I have never given up hope or lashed out at God, even though many times things have seemed very hopeless, and I sometimes felt that He was not there.

I wrote a letter that I read at my daughter's funeral. I hesitated to put this letter in my book, as it had created quite a controversy—not within my family or friends so much, but with my daughter's live-in boyfriend and his family. I wanted everyone to know that this letter was written from my heart—a mother's heart! I had been there from the very beginning of my daughter's life and had loved her and went through many joys and struggles with her. I had loved her longer than anyone else had and had many more thoughts and memories of her than any other person that was there. This was my way of being very honest and open about our relationship and sharing my love and memories of her and also my regrets. My family and friends who had walked this walk with me truly understood where my heart was. A very close clergy friend and his wife read over this letter beforehand. The real names have been changed to respect my children and grandchildren's privacy.

A Letter to My Daughter

As we were going through old photos of you these past few days, it has brought back some wonderful, fun memories for all of us, especially for me, your mom. Being able to remember that we did have some very good fun times together and that we were close in your younger years has helped! Over the many years of troubles, it seemed like many of the good times had been lost. It's been fun remembering our vacations to Wisconsin Dells and to Disney World in Florida. We had very special Christmases and birthday times. You enjoyed Buffy our dog and especially your cat, Snowball! As a little girl, I remembered you were my special little angel and your Daddy's ladybug! You were a little sweetheart and such a joy to have around, but at the same time you were very spoiled and quite the little stinker and really full of it! You could be a little pest to your big sister, Danielle, and your big brother, Shannon. You thought you could get by with anything as long as you gave us a smile! You liked to swing on the tire swing and play in the big sandbox in our backyard. You loved to sing songs and one of your favorites was, "Jesus Loves Me"!

As time went on through the teen years and into your adult life, we had many troubling times that I wish could have been much different. What happened to you as a little girl was not right or fair. When I found out, I tried to understand you and get you the help you needed, but nothing ever seemed to work to make things better for you—and you always blamed me for it happening. I truly am sorry that I couldn't have protected you better; it was my job as your mom to do that, and I'm sorry I didn't know or figure it out. That is truly where the nightmare began for you and our family, and you were never able to get past it. It destroyed so much of your life.

Within this past year, we were seeing some baby steps to things becoming better with our relationship. I wish it could have happened sooner, and we would have had more time. I would have loved the opportunity to have had some good, fun times together as mother and daughter in later years!

We had a special day with you at your oldest daughter Kynnedi's graduation and our fiftieth wedding anniversary party a year ago. This past Christmas was good with you being able to spend the day with your children and our family at our home, after many years being apart. I think you really did enjoy it, and those will be priceless memories for all of us!

I hope deep down inside, you realized how much I loved you, although sometimes it was through tough love and many times from a distance. I am very sorry if that hurt you. Through your struggles, I did learn many things, and even though our relationship was very strained and rocky for many years, I loved being your mom and always hoped for something better. I tried to take a stand for you and reach out to help you, without enabling you—but nothing ever seemed to work or make a difference. I think I wanted more for you than you oftentimes wanted for yourself.

There were a few good times when Kynnedi, your oldest daughter, was a little baby—and things were going better! You did love and take care of her and were a good mom to her until things began falling apart again. I hoped you realized that I really cared and wanted what was best for you and your children. When things got their very worst, I had to take a stand for your children, and I know that upset and hurt you, but I had to do it for them! I hope over time you better understood, and you were beginning to forgive me. All along, I wanted something better for all of us, and I knew it had to be on your terms, when and if you were ready for that. You were truly a survivor—also very stubborn— and maybe that is what kept you going in life.

I prayed for you every day and always wanted the best for you! If that meant we were not a part of your life and were bad memories, I tried to deal with that.

Dad and I hope you had some happiness in your life over the last few years, and from what we are hearing, you have had. You seemed to be doing much better and were a good mom to your youngest daughter, Annie. I also hope you knew God loved you and you felt His presence in your life. I'm so sorry I couldn't have been in —your life—and your youngest daughter's life— as much as I would have wanted to be. Your oldest daughter, Kynnedi, had to be my main focus. I am very glad that you had your little girl, Annie, and her dad and his family, there for you!

I hope and pray that you are in the loving arms of Jesus and at peace now! I also hope that you will have that special time with your grandma and your little boy, Brady, who died so tragically ten days before turning five!

As a mother, I pray and hope that someday we, as a family, will all be together in heaven! Your sudden death shows how quickly things can happen and change; we never know when our final day on earth will be. I pray that each one of us here today will develop a personal rela-tionship with Jesus Christ, knowing Him as our Savior, so we can be assured of where we will be when our time ends here on earth. Knowing and believing that the person you love is in a better place and you will be reunited someday does bring comfort and peace to loved ones left behind. Jesus loves us all and wants us to know Him and experience joy, peace, and love in this life. Eternal life doesn't start when we die—it starts now!

Thank you for the beautiful blessings of your four children still here with us! They are the precious gifts that you have left with us to remember you by. You always were, and forever will be, in my heart—and I trust there will be a day I can hold you in my arms again.

Love You, Mom

My husband and I were hoping to be involved in our youngest granddaughter, Annie's, life, as she was only seven and a half when her mother suddenly died—but her dad and his family did not want this to happen. We were willing to help out in whatever way we could, by watching her while her dad worked or helping with transportation to and from school—also with some financial help if needed. Each month, I have tried to reach out to meet with her, but it has been a struggle and we were never able to see her alone. A handful of times we met for breakfast or lunch, but her dad and other grandma were always there and sometimes others, so we were never able to visit very much and really get to know her or her to know us.

The first year after my daughter's death, I did go to her school two or three times a month to listen to children read in Annie's classroom, and then I would stay to eat lunch with her as she would ask me to. But then her dad stopped that from happening, as I believe he was afraid she might get to know me and maybe even like me. My husband and I had been going to her softball games in the summer—but in the last couple of years her dad would not give me the schedule or her team's name. I eventually figured it out and was able to take in a couple of games.

My husband Paul and I also reached out to a lawyer to try to get once a month visits with our granddaughter set up so my husband and I could get to know her better. At first her dad had agreed, but then never followed through. So we finally just left it alone, and I would just continue monthly to reach out to try to see her. Many times I would never hear back when I would send a message, or my granddaughter's dad would have some excuse as to why we couldn't see her.

I occasionally drop gifts and surprises off at the house for Annie—even a couple surprises at school—hoping that she would get them, but I had to just let things go as I was not going to continue to play games to see her. I always have prayed for her and hope that as she gets older, she will realize and come to know that we have always loved her and wanted to be a part of her life, but we just weren't allowed to be.

I am very grateful that I was able to reconnect, in a small way, with my daughter, Heidi, before her early death. Also, that I always loved her, even though I didn't like many of the things she had done. I encourage parents to always love and pray for your kids and never give up on them! I often wonder, now that she passed away so young, if I had made the right choices as it pertained to Kynnedi's life growing up.

After my daughter's sudden death, I was struggling and asking questions: Where was she? Was she in heaven? She seemed to have walked away from God. But seeing cardinals several days in a row on my husband's red truck in our driveway, plus my devotional readings that week— in addition to *Love Wins* by Rob Bell, which was given to me by a past minister friend, helped to calm me. This book brought me much comfort, and I felt at peace for where she is. If I knew I could see her and hold her again someday, I would be okay. I have to trust now that she is with the Lord in heaven! Later, I learned that a few months before my daughter died, a minister had stopped by her house a couple times to visit with her. God must have been preparing her for what He knew was going to happen!

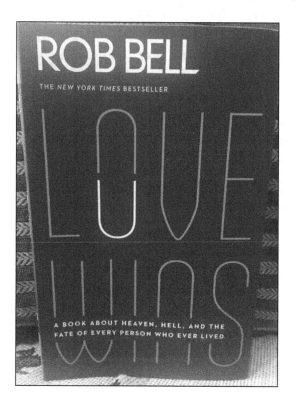

Chapter 9

How Volunteering in My Community Helped Me and Became My Passion

I've always had an interest in volunteering and did a little when my kids were at home. I helped out at their school by being room mother in all my kids' classrooms every year, making special treats on the holidays and going on field trips with them and also some of my grandkid's classrooms. I also would volunteer to help in my children and grandchildren's classrooms by listening to children read or helping with projects or helping with math. I also helped with Girl Scouts and Cub Scouts. I even led a group of six Cub Scout boys for a couple years in our home when my son, Shannon, was younger. I have always loved working with and helping kids!

I also felt I had a better understanding of kids that struggled, having gone through it with a child of my own, who struggled in school and throughout most of her life. As much as I wish my daughter wouldn't have had to go through the struggles she did, I believe I became a better person with more compassion for other children and their parents. It was not fair or right to have to watch my own child be put down and mistreated and to see how we were also treated differently as parents at the school.

For twenty-plus years I taught Sunday school and volunteered at my two churches in many different areas. While being a teacher, I also learned, along with the children, many things about the love of Jesus and the simple ways that Jesus taught and loved!

After my youngest daughter left our home, I felt lead to be a CASA—Court Appointed Special Advocate—and that is my most favorite Passion today! As a CASA, I am a child's voice in the court room for neglected and abused children involved in the child welfare system. I have been a CASA volunteer for over twenty-six years and hope I have made a difference in the lives of the many children I have advocated for and also for their families. One year I was honored with the governor's volunteer award in our state. My decision to become a CASA came about from what I had seen my youngest daughter go through, particularly the sexual abuse. I wanted to help to make a difference bringing about some good for other children and their families and to help better understand them and their needs. My first case was a little girl that had been sexually abused.

I have also served on our local Foster Care Review Board for over ten years, helping to address the needs of children and their families in our area and helping them to get all the services they would need to have a better life! I personally believe parents need to take more responsibility in parenting their children, as that is the most important job they will ever have, as well as our communities need to better understand what many of the children and their parents have gone through with many traumatic experiences in their own lives. When we better understand, by taking time to really listen to them, we can better help children and their parents become successful in helping them to get the appropriate supports and services they need.

I have been involved with many local groups involved with children, such as Community Partnership for Protecting Children and Prevent Child Abuse. I started a local grandparent's support group, advocating many years for grandparents and their grandchildren while my husband and I raised our granddaughter. All through the years and even today, I still get phone calls and try to listen to them and help guide them, as I remember how very hard it is to go through watching little ones you love be caught in the middle of unsafe places, people, and very scary things going on. One year I was surprised to be honored and presented with the Woman of Achievement award, and was even chosen to be the Grand Marshall of our local town parade. I also lead a child abuse awareness walk where my granddaughter, Kynnedi, had the largest team of all!

I am involved in many outreach groups in my community to help others. I help facilitate a Family and Friends Support Group that meets twice a month, helping people who have loved ones addicted to alcohol or drugs, cope with the situation. I had only planned on helping this lady get it started, but after my daughter's death I felt God leading me to stay to help others get through their situations. It has also helped me to move through my situations better and to move on with a more productive life. We read and learned from a book entitled, *Setting Boundaries with Your Adult Children: Six Steps to Hope and Healing for Struggling Parents* by Allison Bottke.

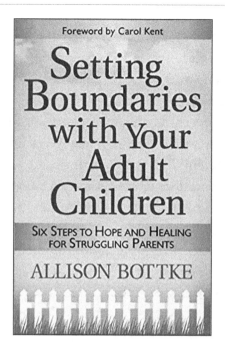

I could have stayed stuck in anger and frustration, but I found God was able to use my disappointments and hurts to help me to better understand and to help others. I believe that is the reason I have gone through some of the things in my life—so that I may better understand others in their struggles, and they can trust that I can feel their desperation, as I have been there myself. It is so very rewarding to reach out and help others! We can always be there to brighten someone's day. Just a smile, a hello, a hug, a phone call, a note sent—or a visit can make a difference to those who are sad or alone, or struggling and having a bad day.

A few years ago, I formed a local private online prayer/devotional group, open to anyone who wanted to be a part, to pray for each other's health needs and concerns and to just be there for one another as friends. We pray for the needs and concerns of our communities and often reach out to help meet those needs. We have become very close, almost like our own little church, and sometimes do meet in person. I have been involved in an online estranged parents' support network around the world. I also have been very involved in a local Anti-Human Trafficking Group, educating our communities to the dangers out there, especially for women and children. I was involved in leading March for our Lives, educating our communities on gun safety! More recently, I became involved with a new jail/prison ministry that was starting, but because of the COVID-19, things have kind of stalled. Hopefully when things move forward, we will be going to area jails and prisons to share Christ's love! I also help with handing out sack lunches to the poor and homeless in our community.

I had been for many years, through my store and church, involved with collecting new shoes and boots to send over to other countries for children in need—also including a note sharing the love of Jesus with them. I have taken two mission trips, one to Romania and the other to Guatemala. The trip to Romania was to visit my husband Paul's family and also to help out a couple of orphanages in that country. We collected many items and money to take over to help them. Most of the money came from one of my local churches. The trip to Guatemala was a small group from my other local church going over to help build a community kitchen for a small village and school there. It was so great to meet and get to know the people of both these countries. They were so genuine and real—and such wonderful loving people—so kind and giving. They had such a strong faith with little or nothing to call their own. We took many things over to give to them—but what they gave us in return was so much more!

My love for God has certainly grown over the many years of my life as I have matured in my faith. I am so very grateful for God's amazing love and His presence in my life and am so very blessed to have my beautiful loving family and my many loyal great friends! Each day I try to be positive and count my blessings! We are to be the hands and feet of Jesus in this hurting world. Everyone can do this—young or old. So let's all put our faith into action! When you experience a nudge from above to help someone or do a good deed, listen! If you are able to hear God's whispers, you've been given a gift! Try to use your gifts to reach out to others and help them. Encourage them to never give up hope! By focusing on others, you get your mind off yourself.

I hope by sharing my story, it will help other parents or grandparents who might be struggling. I pray that others can find the presence of God in their circumstances and learn to count on Him no matter what! I have shared how God has been my Rock and my heavenly Father—and that Jesus is, and has been, my very best Friend who walks beside me each and every day as my Lord and Savior comforting me! The Holy Spirit has been my Advocate to guide and direct me. He speaks to me through my heart. As we learn to trust in the Lord, our hope and faith in Jesus will continuously fill us with confidence.

Chapter 10

Special Memories of My Family

I am so very blessed to have had so many good memories of times with my mother, my sister and my brother—and growing up with their children—my nieces and nephews! We enjoyed spending so many special times and holidays together. We all lived in the same area and saw each other often and got along very well! I am so thankful, as my mother became older and legally blind, that I could be there to help her out and spend some special time with her. I would read to her, share devotions and pray with her, and we made Christmas cards and a scrapbook together. These things seemed to mean a lot to her, and she really enjoyed doing them. My mother was very blessed to have her whole family love her very much and work well together to share in the responsibility of her care, as well as the enjoyment of spending special times together.

There are so many very special memories of my children growing up and their friends also; even though we didn't have a lot of money, we were able to go on many vacations to the Dells when our children were little. We were also able to take two wonderful vacations to Disney World in Florida while they were younger!

I was so excited when our grandchildren were born and would have them over often for fun overnights! The joy of being a grandma is indescribable—you have to become one to truly understand. When the kids were little, we would have tea parties, even the boys, in our basement. They would play downstairs with all the many grandkids' toys we had for them. The kids would build forts with our dining room chairs and blankets in our family room and sleep in there at night. The cousins would have so much fun together. They were so very close. This togetherness helped our granddaughter, Kynnedi, not miss her brothers so much, as they lived so far away. Her cousins became kind of like her brothers.

The kids would get together in the summer, and sometimes our grandsons would be here from the state where they lived. The kids would have so much fun with water balloons and water gun fights in our yard, also blowing bubbles and writing and drawing with chalk on the driveway. They would ride outdoor toys and play and swing on the swing set and trampoline. One time when our grandchildren were younger, they all made special garden stones for my flower garden, which I still treasure and have today.

We often would go to the park, take walks, and go on some special outings out of town. I enjoyed having the kids at our home; oftentimes there would be at least four and sometimes up to seven little ones at once! They would vary in age from four to twelve and I would be exhausted when the weekends were over but was so very happy to have been able to have had them at our home. Sometimes they would make their own pizzas, and at Christmastime we would cut out and decorate cookies. Sometimes my husband wouldn't understand why I would want to have them all, and I would say, "It will only last a few years, and they will be grown up."

As the kids got older, we would get together for pizza and a family fun night on Fridays. We would eat, visit, and play games indoors and out. Baseball was a favorite, with a plastic ball and bat in our backyard! Also, for some we started their own scrapbooks and went to paint ceramics. We had special birthdays and holidays together. Most years, we would take some kind of a family vacation together. This was usually our main Christmas gift to our children and grandchildren—where we would cover lodging and sometimes transportation so all could go. We have all taken a trip to Walt Disney World in Florida. It was such a wonderful time together as we all stayed at the Disney Resort! We have gone to Wisconsin Dells many times, Estes Park, and Denver, Colorado, and also to Branson, Missouri, and Utah several times. Last year we went to Door County, Wisconsin, staying on Sturgeon Bay Lake—which the boys especially loved, with all the things to do on the water: kayaking, boating, and fishing. Fishing was a favorite thing to do for most of our grandsons back at home.

All of our grandsons have been very active in sports and have done very well. Between the six of them, they have covered almost all sports—baseball, basketball, track, cross country, tennis, bowling, golf, football, and taekwondo. One of our older grandsons took first place in his division at State Cross Country. He is an awesome runner! Our granddaughter participated in choir and band and also played some golf and ran track in school. My husband and I tried to attend as many events as we could. Many times, we were at an event almost every week night, and we loved being able to go.

As the kids are growing up now, it is somewhat harder to all get together. Our three far-away grandsons are closer now, so it will make it easier to plan get togethers with them. Our granddaughter finished up college and recently got married. We are so very proud of her and all her many accomplishments. She has definitely been a success story, overcoming many things that happened in her young life. It is unbelievable we have come to this time so fast! My daughter Danielle and I try to get away two or three times a year for a weekend, and I treasure these times just having mother-daughter time. My mother and her sister, and my sister, Sandy and me, used to do fun overnights, also. We also try to get together as a family for a meal every month or so for whoever can work it out.

As a grandmother looking back through the years, I am so very happy my grandchildren were around, and I was able to be actively involved in their lives so much! The rewards of having grandchildren is amazing! I love it when they get together now, sometimes playing cards and other times just sitting around talking and remembering all the fun times they've had together! They all are so very close to one another. I take lots of pictures and make each one of them at least one scrapbook for their graduation. I wish that I could name each one of them and show pictures of them, as I am so very proud of each one and love them all very much! Through the years, I had special dolls made to represent each one of my children and grandchildren when they were little. I have many special Scripture messages and sayings throughout my home about my family and my grandchildren. I have also treasured, throughout the years, the many cards I have received from my children and grandchildren! They meant so very much to me at the time, and they still do today. I must take after my mom, as she always loved the cards she received from her children and grandchildren.

Families are like branches on a tree. We all grow in different directions yet our roots remain as one. For this family, we are grateful. Family is not an important thing; It is everything. Remember, as far as anyone knows we are a nice, normal family. Family is a compass that guides us. Family: we may not have it all together, but together we have it all. Even a family tree has some sap. Having a place to go is a home. Having someone to love is a family. Having both is a blessing. If you met my family you would understand. Love makes a family. The best is yet to come. Other things may change but we start and end with family. We are blessed.

I may not be
rich or famous,
but I do have
PRICELESS
GRANDCHILDREN

GRANDCHILDREN
are the reward you get
for not strangling
your teenagers

A Special Prayer for You!

- I pray you take time to realize the sacrifice that Jesus made for You, suffering and dying a horrible death on the Cross, for your Salvation!
- Take time to PRAY each day and Thank Him for the many Blessings you have!
- I pray you will be filled with His Holy Spirit and feel God's Presence and Love, and Joy and Peace, in Your Life.
- I pray you will spend time with God, Your Father, in His Word, the Bible and in His Church Just like we want our kids to spend time with us, so does God want His children to spend time with Him and show our Love and Thankfulness!
- I Pray you learn and Live God's first and most important Commandment "You must love the Lord your God with all your heart, all your soul, and all your mind!"
- I pray that you will be the Light of Jesus to Others! Be the example of Jesus to your Children, future Grandchildren, and Goals!
- I pray you will ask yourself "What would Jesus think or want me to do" in making decisions. Do I know for sure where I will be tomorrow, if I don't wake up?
- God Loves His Children and wants the Best possible Life for all of them, here and Now, and for all eternity. Don't miss what God has to offer You, Today and Forever!

I so much wish our youngest daughter could have lived longer and been able to play more of a part in her children's lives and the rest of our family. She missed out on so very much. I'm so happy that she did have the opportunity to go on to have another little girl, Annie, who she was able to take care of and enjoy some, as she was only seven years old when her mother died. I always knew that my daughter had a kind, loving heart and could be a good mom. It is so sad that our oldest granddaughter Kynnedi (whom we raised) and our youngest granddaughter, Annie, both only had their mom in their lives until they were seven years old.

We continue to want to be involved with our youngest granddaughter who is now eleven, but her dad continues to not want to work with us in order for us to have a relationship with her. As I mentioned a little earlier, we did legally look at this—because of our daughter Heidi's death, we did have some grandparent's rights—but not having had an earlier relationship with Annie kept us from moving forward much with those rights.

I have tried many times and in many ways to have a once a month meeting with our youngest granddaughter to get together for a meal with her dad present—but many times her dad has continued to be uncooperative. It would have taken her dad working with us, at first, for her to feel comfortable with us alone—but he didn't seem to want to allow us to form a grandparent relationship with her. We have seen our granddaughter only a handful of times, and those times have mostly been out in public. I have come to finally realize that her dad will never allow us to form a grandparent-grandchild relationship with her. Our daughter had probably shared with him a lot of negativity, blaming us for losing her children. This is so very sad, as I truly feel that my daughter Heidi would have wanted us to be a part of her little girl's life, especially since she isn't here now for her own daughter. Our relationship had been moving toward a better place, and I believe this would have continued if she were alive today. I had talked to her on the phone five days before she died, as she had called to thank me for a gift I had dropped by for Annie.

I have had to just pray and give this to the Lord, as there is nothing more I can do. I just continue to reach out to my granddaughter Annie's dad once a month, asking if we can meet for an hour on their schedule and any place they want, treating them to breakfast or lunch, but I have not had real good results. I believe our granddaughter has been told, or has overheard, negative things about us. That is so sad all the way around, as I believe kids can never have enough love from their family! I will never give up hope that someday this could change.

Chapter 11

Looking Back over My Life

As I look back over my life, I have seen the hand of God watching over, protecting, and intervening in my life and in the lives of my children and grandchildren! Many times I did not realize or see that happening at the time; it is only as I look back that I can see that He was always there!

I feel so very blessed for the fifty-four years I have had with my husband and the fact that we have grown closer over the years. God has certainly worked so many times in our lives. My husband used to get agitated easily and not be able to relax, but I believe God has been working in his life, allowing him to calm down and enjoy life more. Being able to retire, years ago—and less stressful days—have also helped! We are also very thankful for our good health.

Although we have shared much sadness in our lives, the joys have outweighed the disappointments and sad times. We have been richly blessed with our now-adult children and grand-children! As much as I would have wished to never have gone through all the hurt and pain we have or have had to see our daughter and her children go through, I believe I am a much better person because of it! I believe I have more empathy and understanding for others because of what I have gone through. We can thrive in every season of our lives, whether good or bad, if we are willing to trust God, even though we don't see or understand. We need to walk by faith, not sight! (2 Cor. 5:7). We can find that God is faithful in every season. I also believe that God has used me, throughout these years, to be able to help, reach out, and to better understand others! I believe that God can speak to us through our circumstances, through people, and during quiet times with Him! We just need to be still, wait, and listen!

My daughter's life, I believe, exhibited how childhood trauma can affect and destroy so much of a person's life and their future. So sad! Heidi's life was like a mystery to try to unravel. I always hoped someday she could have completely opened up and shared her own story, as I believe there was much more than I even knew about. She always left enough notes for me to find as she always knew I would look into things. I also found a video tape she had made of herself. Was she trying to tell the story of what happened to her? Her therapist at the time felt she was doing so well that maybe it wasn't a good time to approach her with the tape, as she felt she might regress. Of course, she soon turned eighteen and left our home, so this was never looked into. Sadly I could never put all the pieces together, and now she has gone to her grave with her secrets that will never be told. She was definitely a survivor, but her soul and spirit had been damaged by what had happened to her. I once read a very good book that helped me to understand sexual abuse better and how sexual abuse can destroy the soul of the person that it has happened to. The name of the book was, *A Wounded Heart: Hope for Adult Victims of Childhood Sexual Abuse*, by Dr. Dan B. Allender. As a mom, that seemed to be what I saw had happened to my sweet child! I also want to encourage those with young children to make things be surprises in your home and family—versus secrets—as people who want to harm little children will tell them to keep secrets.

I'm hoping by sharing all of this that I'm giving people a little insight into how many children could be living in homes where the parents' past traumas, mental illness, and addictions are challenges in the children's lives. Imagine if these were your kids or grandkids living in these situations; how would you feel and what would you do or want others to do? Many times, it takes deeper looking into situations and becoming more involved to really see the whole picture. Parents in these situations can be very manipulative and clever, putting their children at even greater risks. Adult childhood experiences (ACEs) are events and traumas occurring before the age of eighteen. ACEs include all types of abuse and neglect as well as parental mental illness, alcoholism, substance use, divorce, incarceration, and domestic violence. If a child has had four or more of these happen in their early years, they run the risk of having many problems in their adult life. The more they have encountered, the higher the risks are!

I also hope we have learned that the anger that we see in people is often from the deep hurts they have experienced. Hurt people tend to hurt other people. Maybe if we would take more time to listen to people and also open ourselves up a little to them, helping them to see we are not perfect and that we have also struggled in areas, they might be more apt to open up and talk more freely. When we build friendships and can grow to trust one another, maybe we can help move through the hurts and anger to a better understanding. Many times, family members are too close to the situation to really be the ones to help when things are off the track, so others may be the ones that could make that difference. Could it be you?

I have also questioned over the years if past generational sins of addictions in my family were showing up in my children and whether I could have even stopped some things from happening. I probably might have gone overboard on getting to the point of not having any alcohol in my home, but I had seen so much hurt and pain caused to my family from the use of alcohol. I have nothing against an occasional drink; it's just how people handle it that makes the difference!

I encourage those of you who have addictive families to take the time to look seriously and honestly at addictions in your families and try to talk honestly and openly about this with younger people to help educate them. I actually believe it's important to start to talk with them much younger than I did, before the teen years, in order that they might be more open to listening to you! Kids from addictive backgrounds run much higher risks to becoming addicted easier—the younger they start, the higher the risk—sometimes even with a first drink! I have found that our society is so accepting of young people drinking and that it is accepted as the norm. Many parents allow underage drinking in their own homes with their kids and their friends. From my personal experience in my family, it looked like it was every other generation falling more with the males becoming addicted. Please never give up the fight to break addictions in your family!

God has definitely been a big part of this long journey, and He has taken what was meant for bad, what could have destroyed me and my husband and our marriage, and used it for good! As my husband and I were talking a couple days ago, we agreed that we have grown closer to each other and to the Lord through the trials in our lives—and so maybe we were the luckier ones. Always remember God is an awesome God, able to intervene and lift you up no matter what! I pray that God, the source of hope, will fill you completely with His joy and peace because you trust in Him (Rom. 15:13). You will never be sorry in reaching out to God for His amazing love and for His help and support!

I have for the most part tried to enjoy life to the fullest! We have never had a lot of money, and have lived in our modest older home for almost forty years, but I believe my life has been full of many good things with all my needs met and many extras. I also believe my children had all the necessities and many extras. I tried to raise my children to love God and to treat others with respect and kindness. I want my children and grandchildren to be happy in life, but I don't think happiness necessarily comes from having a lot of money. Happiness comes from having a relationship with the Lord and finding the purpose He has for your life—and reaching out and caring and giving yourselves to others! Be willing to venture out of your comfort zone and try new things that God might be leading you to do. Don't be afraid, as He will go with you! God is a good God, and He is still in charge.

God blessed my husband and me with enough resources to have done great things with what we had. We have always tithed to our churches that we attended; even when I thought we might struggle, God has always provided us with enough money to pay our bills and live comfortably. I feel I have shared with many people my time and resources. We were able to sponsor children from outside our country to give them a better life and help them to know Jesus Christ, as well as give to many local needs!

If I could go back, I would want my husband and me to have truly put God in the center of our marriage and our family. We went to church as a family, and our kids always went to Sunday school. We shared prayers each day at lunch and dinner and prayers at bedtime and would read devotions, but as I look back, I wish we could have been more connected in a more personal relationship with the Lord, letting Him lead us. Also, I would have wanted both my husband and me to have worked more together in the parenting of our children. Being a parent is the hardest job you will ever have and the job that you will love the most! Enjoy each day with your children for they will go by fast.

My biggest disappointments in my life were that I never really had a dad who was much involved in my life. As years have brought better understanding of him, I still feel I missed a lot by not having a dad there to really care about me as his little girl and make me feel special—and also our family being broken by the divorce of my parents. I tell others that have had involved dads to be so very thankful for their dad's love and involvement in their lives! I'm also very sorry for the tragic things that went on with my youngest daughter, Heidi, and her children and the young death of my first grandson. Our daughter was robbed of so much joy and happiness in her life—first by others, and then later by the poor decisions she made. I wish, as her mother, that I could have saved her from all of this heartache.

I have never had a higher education, only graduating from high school, and I often wish I would have went on to some college. However, I feel I have accomplished great things in my life—the most important being a mom and a grandma! I have tried to give my life to God and let Him use me. I believe our hearts should break for what breaks the heart of God. I have found that when you reach out to care about others, you are deeply rewarded. I have become more outspoken and bolder in my older years, which has often gotten me into some trouble—especially in the church! I have tried to speak to and do what is right, standing up in my church and also my community for the injustices that I see.

I am so very thankful that my husband and I have stayed together through the seriously tough times in our lives and that our marriage made it to this point in our golden years. God has certainly been at work through it all! He can take our messes in our lives and bring some good out of them. And yes, you can find peace in the mess! We have attained contentment and happiness—and joy! Happiness depends on your circumstances, but joy is rooted in your identity—in how Jesus loves and sees you—and walks with you. Joy is not the same as happiness or excitement, but rather a deep satisfaction that comes from being in step with God and His perfect will. "The joy of the Lord is your strength" (Neh. 8:10). We are not rich, but we have enough money to not worry about money and are rich in what is important in life! Praise be to God!

I have many wonderful, fond memories of our family vacations and my husband and my bus trips and vacations. On our bus trips we have been able to visit beautiful Niagara Falls, Mackinac Island, Washington, D.C., and New York City. As I write this, we are on a month's vacation in Alabama. I feel so very blessed and thankful for the privilege and opportunity to be able to have a condo right on the Gulf of Mexico, looking out at the peaceful relaxing water. As we walk on the white beach and I look out at the waters, I feel God's presence, love, and peace! It is probably the closest I will feel to heaven from earth. We saw three dolphins swimming close to the shore right out back from our condo as we walked a while ago.

I have been very involved in church for most of my adult life, and that has been very important to me! After marrying and having my children and being a longtime member of two different churches, being very involved on many different committees, I have been very disappointed in what I have seen over the years and the deep hurts I have experienced as well as seen done to others that I cared about, including ministers and their families. I have seen Christians, inside and outside the church, treat each other in very unchristian, hurtful ways. I have come to better understand why so many people say they don't want to be involved in a church! I have heard sermons and read from the Bible what Jesus wants us to do, but oftentimes see that we really don't want to do those things, such as feed the hungry, reach out to the poor and homeless, and welcome the refugees!

We seem to want people to be put together before we really want them to join our midst and really include them, or we look at what money they might be able to bring instead of being the church—a helpful support for them first. I personally think we need to reach out to our communities and neighborhoods more, getting to know the people, the lonely and lost, the addicted and the homeless to get to really know them and their deep hurts and needs. Then and only then will they want to join us at our churches! We need to really sincerely care about *all* people! We need to do more listening and reaching out and including and doing what Jesus tells us we are to do—loving them like Jesus! We need to remember that Jesus forgives and Jesus loves, no matter what. While praying is very important, we must be willing to take some major action steps! By just telling someone that is hungry, afraid, or homeless that you will pray for them without trying to do more to help them fulfill their immediate needs just makes us feel good, not them. As James 2:26 says, "Faith is dead without good works!"

Over the years, I have seen the powerful, the wealthy, and the educated pretty much control final decisions made in churches. A lot of politics seem to go on in many churches also, which can cause much division. What would Jesus say about this? Weren't His disciples just plain ordinary men? Wouldn't Jesus be walking beside the weary and the down and out? Jesus says that we are to be "His Light" in this dark world—His hands and feet! People often will say, "Where is God today? Why doesn't He do something?" If we are His followers and disciples, aren't we supposed to be the ones doing something? Doesn't God expect that of us if we are His followers? Aren't we to be the church out in the world? I have never walked away from God or my faith, but I have been very disheartened to what I have seen and have left a couple of churches because of some of those things.

Right now we are in the middle of the coronavirus, and people are so frightened and afraid. I pray they will draw close to the Lord through this time and realize that everyone is important in the eyes of God! I sit here in my warm home, where light snow is falling, on my seventy-second birthday amidst the coronavirus. I'm feeling very thankful and blessed to have had my children and grandchildren share a couple hours together with me, but I am missing the hugs I want to give them as we keep our distance. I also pray for and realize that there are many people that aren't so fortunate to have a warm home and family, and I'm saddened for them.

My granddaughter is planning a wedding during this, not knowing if she will be able to have it. I do trust that we will get through this, but I'm sure it will be a while before we are on the other side of this. I just hope that we all can come out better because of this and grow closer to the God who is in charge! I pray for our country and the world as we go through this. Everyone is frightened and scared, not knowing what the future holds for their physical health and their financial security. I pray that those who know Jesus as their Savior feel His loving comforting arms around them! For those who don't know Jesus—I pray that they come to know Him through these very trying times. God, we need to trust that You have the whole world in your hands! I also hope that we go deeper in our understanding of one another and will take a stand to want to make a difference so that all people will feel loved and treated justly, no matter the color of their skin, where they come from, their educational status, if they are rich or poor, or who they choose to love!

If anyone wants to know Jesus more personally, go to the Bible—His words! Seek out a church and faithful people to go to and connect with those that truly love Him! For anyone reading this book, God can walk with you if you invite Him to! Psalm 46:1 says, "God is our Refuge and Strength—always ready to help in times of trouble!" We need to be trusting God's love, wisdom, and power above our own. He always wants our best and knows what is best for us!

I have finally made my own prayer room after seeing the movie, *War Room*. I have wanted to do this for so long, and I find it to be a very relaxing, peaceful place where I can go to be alone with God. I have my maternal grandmother's old rocking chair to sit on (pictured on the cover), and this is where I often read my Bible and do my devotions. I am reminded of all the times I have rocked my children and grandchildren. In the warmer months, I love to sit out on my patio (designed and completed by two of my grandsons) in the early morning, reading my devotions, listening to the birds sing, and watching the squirrels and our friendly little chipmunk scamper across the patio. I enjoy and love walking in nature and find that listening to praise and worship music connects me to the Lord! Also I have found that journaling my thoughts and talking with God in that way has been very helpful to me. I also love to read and learn new things. I am a very sentimental person and special people and things mean a lot to me. Throughout my home, I have many reminders of God's love. I am thankful God can use me to be there for others, as I was able to be there for my good friend when she suddenly lost her son, helping her through the unbelievable pain.

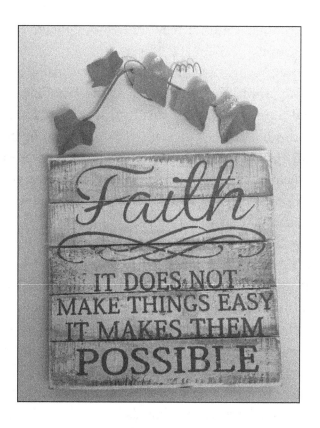

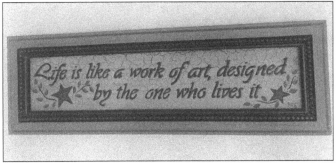

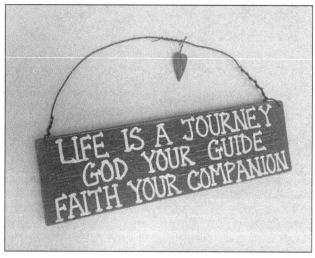

For a few years, I have been spending time with God first thing every morning for about a half hour or more, and it has been a great way to get my day started right! Recently my husband has even been joining me in some of my morning devotion time. Try to make time to spend at least five minutes alone in quite time with God to breathe, listen, and hear His voice. What is He saying to you? What is He asking you to do? God can use you for a much bigger purpose than just for yourself. Try drawing closer to Him and see what happens. What might He be calling You to do today?

We can come to Jesus just as we are to thank Him, to tell Him we love Him, and to ask Him for the needs and desires of our heart. We do not have to have perfect prayers. What matters is our heart, not a certain way that we pray, where we pray, or how many words we speak. Listen to what God wants to speak or say to you today! "Be Still and Know that I am God" (Ps. 46:10). He can bring you comfort and strength and give you hope and an exciting life! To grow in your relationship with God, walk with Him daily, trust Him daily, and worship Him daily! Let Jesus's light shine through you so others will want to know who He is!

My Grandmother's rocking chair sits in a corner of my prayer room, where I often sit to do my devotions in the morning.

This beautiful picture is on another wall of my prayer room. This room is my special place to go to for doing many things! I find it to be a very comforting, peaceful place to be alone with God—to read and relax—and also to work on my computer and do zoom meetings during this time.

I always thought being a Christian meant my life would be easy as I walked with the Lord through my life. Boy, was I wrong! I have to laugh now, after maturing in my faith and seeing what I have learned and what God promises us. He doesn't promise us an easy walk through life, but He does promise us that He will always be there for us, and He will carry us when we think we can't go on another minute. Then, when we truly trust and love Him with our whole heart and give our life to Him, He will often use our worst hurt or pain to be a part of reaching out to help others going through their worst hurt and pain. It's hard to understand it until you let go and let God work in your life! Instead of blaming God and others for all your woes, let go and let God use you to be that light in the darkness for someone else. Give a smile and a hello to people you meet; yes, even to strangers you don't know! We can train our minds to focus on the good and use our words to verbalize the good, realizing that our words do have the power to change people's lives. God can and will work things out for our ultimate good!

I have found that throughout my many years, I have found shelter and rest in the loving arms of Jesus who gave me comfort, hope, and His peace. How could I have peace and joy and be thankful among the storms and crazy times in my life? Only through the love of Jesus! I am so very grateful for His grace and His forever presence. I have learned that gratitude is the gateway to peace and that His grace is in the very center of our gratitude. I've learned to take one day at a time and truly enjoy each day—finding the good and the blessings even in the not so good days! I believe I have learned, as an older person, to slow down and take breaks along the way, savoring the moments of life, for time passes so very quickly! Treasure those family get togethers! Reconnect and strengthen friendships! I am very blessed to have many lifelong friends whom I treasure—I could not have made it through my life without them. Make sure you enjoy the little things in life, for they will become the big things and the most important things in the end!

Remember God loves you and wants you to be a part of His family! God saves all who trust in Him, so give your life to Him today and love Him and Love others! Joy comes when you do! Joy is the infallible sign of the presence of God! Without God leading us, life is unable to be truly lived.

Thank You, Lord, for Your love—the joy and hope You bring me—and Your forever presence in my life!
God's richest blessings, love, and peace to all of you who read this book!

—Darcie Joy

P.S. Our granddaughter did get married! Her church wedding changed because of COVID within a couple weeks of the wedding, from a guest list of two-hundred and fifty people down to ten people—and then allowing up to—seventy people within four days of the wedding. We had to scurry to get everyone notified (no reception of course). It turned out beautiful with a surprise car parade for them. I am very proud of her as she seems to be able to stay calm during the disappointments and storms of her life and she can let God guide and direct her.

Also, to keep life exciting, we got a puppy for Christmas! She's a bundle of energy and joy!

About the Author and Acknowledgments

I believe God has used my trials to make me a stronger and better person. I hope those reading this book will find that God works in many ways throughout your life to bring you closer to Him, if you will let Him, and can turn you into a better more loving, caring, and understanding person. He can also turn your tragedies into triumphs! I tried to write honestly and openly about my feelings in this book, without going into all of the very personal details, but I have included enough details so those reading this book will understand how serious things were for many years. The many times when things seemed so very hopeless for me in my life were when I had to rely and trust in Jesus to get me through each day!

I have been back and forth for several years whether I should write this book or not and what I should include, but I have felt God leading me to share my story, and while writing I felt lead to share even more. I wanted to share as truthfully as I could what I remember and have journaled over the years. As I have grown over many years in my faith, I have learned to trust God more and more throughout my life! "Faith does not make things easy, but it makes them possible" (Luke 1:37). It is not easy to let go of things, but when you can give it to God, He can lower your stress level and bring about calm and peace and also some joy in your life! It is truly amazing how God has worked in my life through many happy times and probably, most of all, through the unfortunate tragic times of my life. I am so very grateful for His love for me and His love and protection for my loved ones!

I love and believe in Jesus Christ as my Savior and God's one and only Son. I do believe and better understand today how His Holy Spirit lives and works in and through me and how I can listen and work with Him to make a difference in my life and in the lives of my family, friends, and others. It has taken me many years to really fully understand the Trinity—the three in one—God as Father, Jesus as Son, and the Holy Spirit as my Advocate. I have finally grown to realize and better understand how God can definitely work in many mysterious ways!

I always believed that Jesus loved me, but it was in my trials that He became more personal and real to me. It was through the very tough times—when I felt so alone and that no one understood me—that Jesus became my first Love and my very best Friend! I could feel His comforting, loving arms around me in my pain and aloneness. I also learned what it has meant to really "let go and let God." Over the years I have learned to trust God and to better understand He knows what is best for me and my loved ones! I learned to find peace in the mess of my life. I would also hope that each one of my loved ones will come to know Jesus and His love for them in this real close personal way and remember that they are never alone, no matter what they are going through in their own lives. Life can be tough, but God is always good and still is in charge. I also have found out that oftentimes my prayers have been answered much differently than I prayed for.

To my precious children, grandchildren, and my husband. I love you with all of my heart! I wish I could name each one of you and show photos of you because I am so very proud of you, but you know who you are. I will have one of my Bibles for each one of you with special verses and messages inside. I hope each of you will treasure this Bible, after I'm gone, and grow closer to the Lord throughout your life. My author name has included all of you by using either your first, middle, or last initials. For the sake of privacy, I have chosen to use fictitious names. I truly do not want my children or grandchildren to be embarrassed or hurt, in any way, by my sharing my story. I want my youngest daughter's children to know (especially my oldest granddaughter) how very much I loved their mom and cared about her, even though sometimes it didn't seem to look that way. Also, that their mother loved them, but because of her own pain and issues wasn't able to care for them in the way that she should have-- and I'm very sorry for that. I feel led to share how the Lord has given me wisdom, strength, and guidance in my most desperate times to carry me through. I want you all to know that I have always wanted the very best life for each one of you! I have prayed for each of you every day and have asked God to surround you with His love and protection! This is a prayer I would often pray for all of you as you grew older.

> You know all that is in my heart, Dear God,
> and so you know how much I love and care
> about my children and grandchildren. I want
> to entrust them to Your care that You might

guide them in their daily decisions and keep them from harm. Help me to believe that You watch over them always and that You want only good things for them. Forgive them when they fail and keep Your guiding hand on them as they face the big and little decisions of their lives. I place them in Your loving care! Amen.

Each one of you has been my joy in life and often my purpose for living—sometimes maybe too much! We have gone through many happy, fun times and also some very hurtful sad times together as a family. Please forgive me if you were hurt by anything I ever said or did, as it certainly wasn't my intention. I hope that you can take the many good things about our family and then improve on what could be made better in your own family. I am very proud of the responsible adult children and the good parents you are—and so very grateful to be able to watch my grandchildren grow to become teens and young adults and be able to see all of you often and be so involved in your lives.

I have also come to better understand why things might happen, as I have learned about past trauma, addictions, sexual abuse, and adverse childhood experiences (ACEs). I realize they play a big role in the pain and struggles of so many individuals and families and the hardships of trying to overcome these traumas! I believe my youngest daughter's life, exhibited how childhood trauma had affected and destroyed so much of her young life and her future. Addictions and mental illness are often intertwined, as well as sexual abuse. I hope that everyone that reads this book realizes that I truly loved my youngest daughter, but over time, I couldn't understand her thinking at all nor was I able to help her—which broke my heart.

I encourage family members to not enable loved ones in your families. Love them, but hold them accountable, and let God take over and heal them. We *can* choose to *stop* the cycle of alcohol addictions in our own families! In the Bible, it does say that the sins of the father go back to the third and fourth generations, and I do believe there is much truth in this. I have seen it over generations in my own family. I always thought how unfair it was for God to punish those who were just born into families and situations, but I have learned that anyone can *stop* the cycle of addiction in their own family and work to start and create a new path for future generations to come. It might not be easy, but I think it can be done! "I can do all things through Christ who strengthens me" (Phil. 4:13). Oftentimes, a family needs to get out of the way for God to be able to work in a loved one's life!

I'm so very thankful that Jesus has sent me a wonderful, loving, caring family—and so many loving faithful friends. Again, I wish I could name each of you, but you know who you are. You have all walked beside my husband and me during many difficult years with love and understanding. Sometimes things don't turn out the way you would want them to or have planned and prayed—but I believe God knows what is best, and He will get you through anything! Romans 8:28 says, "And we know that all things work together for good to them that love God, to them who are called according to His purpose." Trust Jesus to place you right where you need to be!

"Just trust Me," God says,
"and see what I can do!"

For anyone needing support or wanting to
correspond with me, I can be reached at
darciejoymiller10@gmail.com